PRAISE FOR *UNRULY*

"On these pages, Shelah is the voice of our best friend, holding up a mirror to our faces while sharing her transformative testimony and radical wisdom, inviting us to be honest about how we got here and what we are willing to be unwavering about to get to our highest imaginations of ourselves. *Unruly* will ask you to 'Become.' And so you will."

EBONYJANICE
author of *All the Black Girls Are Activists*

"If you are looking for a nuanced, bold, and clearly outlined approach to adorning yourself in your unique crown of Black excellence that you were born with but often stripped of, this book will live on your nightstand. Additionally, for those who are a part of or allies to the Black community, who are seeking to understand how to love Black women within their realities to their highest potential, *Unruly* is an invaluable resource."

SHAN BOODRAM
sex and relationship expert on Netflix's *Too Hot to Handle*

"What Shelah is doing with *Unruly* is truly groundbreaking! Through her transparency and vulnerability, she invites us on a journey of honesty and reflection. She challenges us to give ourselves permission to change our minds about who we thought we were and who we thought we had to be. Shelah serves as a model of rebellion and growth, and that guides us as we journey through our own healing. As a therapist, I love and appreciate the radical approach to healing and authenticity that *Unruly* provides!"

DR. EBONY
creator of *My Therapy Cards*

"In *Unruly*, Shelah Marie offers exactly the kind of no-nonsense and loving advice you'd expect from a big sister or longtime friend. Filled with deeply personal stories, thoughtful questions, and actionable steps, this is a beautiful guide that will no doubt inspire and motivate young women for years to come."

FRANCHESCA RAMSEY
creator and host of *MTV Decoded* and author
of *Well, That Escalated Quickly*

"In *Unruly*, Shelah unapologetically highlights the grace and power of Black womanhood, delivering a transformative guide to self-discovery and embracing authenticity. This book is a beacon of inspiration and essential reading for anyone looking to own their truth and uncover their resilience and power."

JUSTIN MICHAEL WILLIAMS
author of *Stay Woke*

"With *Unruly*, Shelah provides a road map for undoing all that we have been taught we need to be, do, and perceive to earn the title of 'good' as a Black woman. This book doesn't just talk about what it means to be authentic to self—the exercises guide the reader through tangible ways to experience and embody the concepts discussed. Shelah demonstrates her commitment to freedom of the everyday Black woman with this work. It's not just about the 'talk' but also in 'action.'"

MELISSA IFILL, LCSW
therapist and coach

"Shelah's knack for bridging wellness with approachability is something that women of color have searched for, far and wide. Shelah doesn't preach at you; she walks with you. *Unruly* is the permission slip, and cerebral bus ticket, to your next level of understanding self. For those looking for a safe space to do the work—pull up a seat."

EVITA ROBINSON
writer and founder of NOMADNESS Travel Tribe

UNRULY

ALSO BY SHELAH MARIE

Positive You:
A Personal Growth Journal for Women

A Guide to Reclaiming Your True Self

SHELAH MARIE

BOULDER, COLORADO

Sounds True
Boulder, CO

© 2024 Shelah Marie

Sounds True is a trademark of Sounds True Inc.
All rights reserved. No part of this book may be used or reproduced in any manner without written permission from the author(s) and publisher.

No AI Training: Without in any way limiting the author's and publisher's exclusive rights under copyright, any use of this publication to "train" generative artificial intelligence (AI) technologies to generate text is expressly prohibited. The author reserves all rights to license uses of this work for generative AI training and development of machine learning language models.

Published 2024

Book design by Ranee Kahler

Printed in Canada

BK06650

Library of Congress Cataloging-in-Publication Data

Names: Marie, Shelah, author.
Title: Unruly : a guide to reclaiming your true self / Shelah Marie.
Description: 1 edition. | Boulder, CO : Sounds True, Inc, [2024]
Identifiers: LCCN 2024010910 (print) | LCCN 2024010911 (ebook) | ISBN 9781649630773 (hardback) | ISBN 9781649630780 (ebook)
Subjects: LCSH: Self-acceptance. | Self-confidence. | Self-actualization (Psychology)
Classification: LCC BF575.S37 M365 2024 (print) | LCC BF575.S37 (ebook) |
DDC 158.1--dc23/eng/20240509
LC record available at https://lccn.loc.gov/2024010910
LC ebook record available at https://lccn.loc.gov/2024010911

To little girls everywhere who were told they were too much.
May she be heard, seen, and validated.
And to the women in my world who are committed to creating
a safer, gentler world for us,
Thank you for being on this journey with me.
May we all live our truest story.

"let her be born / let her be born / & handled warmly."

—Ntozake Shange,
*For Colored Girls Who Have Considered Suicide /
When the Rainbow Is Enuf*

Contents

Introduction: It Was Time for a New Story . . . 1

Understand

Chapter 1 The World Is Your Stage . . . 13

Chapter 2 Setting the Scene for Safety . . . 25

Unconfirmed

Chapter 3 Becoming Unbecoming . . . 45

Chapter 4 Main Character Energy . . . 55

Unperform

Chapter 5 Compassionate Character Study . . . 83

Chapter 6 Self-Love in Action . . . 95

Chapter 7 Passed-Down Performances . . . 107

Chapter 8 Presence Over Presenting . . . 117

Chapter 9 What's Your Next Scene?: Serious Daydreaming . . . 131

Chapter 10 Casting for Companionship: Be Different. Together. . . . 143

Unfixed

Chapter 11 A Dramatic Pause: Please Sit Your Ass Down Somewhere . . . 175

Chapter 12 Keep Your Seams Visible: The Beauty Is in the Stitching . . . 187

Bonus Metta Meditation Exercise (Based on a Teaching by Steven Smith) . . . 193

Notes . . . 199

About the Author . . . 205

Introduction

It Was Time for a New Story

If I had to choose a moment in my life that kick-started my healing journey, it would be that Friday night in my Brooklyn brownstone apartment when I got into an argument with the man I thought would be my husband. I know astrology is a very complex language and it's not wise to overgeneralize a sign, but for the sake of this conversation, I'm going to make a sweeping generalization here and say that Aries like to move swiftly. We are known as the infants of the zodiac, so imagine a determined toddler trying their best to walk even though they don't have the proper motor skills yet. One Aries in a relationship is enough to drive things forward at a pace that could give anyone whiplash, so imagine the situation I found myself in as an Aries *dating* an Aries. I just knew he was my husband; it didn't matter that I'd only known him for a few weeks. But I soon found out that his fire and my fire created chaos.

At a certain point it became clear that I needed to leave the relationship, which was not an easy decision because I loved him very much and I knew the conversation wasn't going to go over well.

Leading up to that night, I rehearsed my breakup monologue, just like I would rehearse my lines for an audition. I had recorded it as a voice note and listened to it on the train ride to and from work. I rehearsed what I thought would be the gentlest and kindest way to end a relationship. To be fair, looking back, he probably didn't perceive it as kind, but that was my intention and what I was aiming for, even if I didn't quite hit the mark.

Despite us having an on-again, off-again relationship for the past few months, the breakup still came as a shock to him. He was livid. At the time, I was living with roommates, who were home from work during the breakup. One roommate was in the kitchen entertaining a friend and, based on the engaging laughs between the clinking of dishes, I figured they were having a chill, enjoyable dinner. In an attempt not to disturb their evening, I tried to do the breakup as discreetly as possible, but I knew there was no way to do it perfectly.

"I think we need to go our separate ways," I said matter-of-factly. "And you can't stay here anymore. You don't have to leave right now, but—"

Before I could finish my sentence, he was already frantically gathering his stuff and preparing to leave the apartment. He proceeded to move his things out—*at that moment*—one trip downstairs at a time. With each trip downstairs, the tension grew. He started hurling insults, and I felt things beginning to escalate. I didn't know it then, but due to an unstable upbringing, I had been trained to attune to other people's behavior. Our fights were typically dirty, and I didn't want to be that version of myself at that moment. I didn't want to hurt him or myself any more than I already had. I also feared that any reaction from me would warrant an explosive response on his part, and on top of all that, I was trying to be mindful of my roommates and their guests. So instead of engaging, I put in some headphones and picked up where I had left off on the audiobook of *Radical Forgiveness* by Colin Tipping, a book my now-ex-boyfriend had recommended to me.

"The beauty of Radical Forgiveness lies in the fact that it does not require us to recognize what we project. We simply forgive the person for what is happening at the time. In doing so, we automatically undo the projection, no matter how complicated the situation. The reason for this is simple, in that the person represents the original pain that caused us to project in the first place. As we forgive him or her, we clear that original pain," Tipping said.

Underneath those words, I could hear the sharp tone of my ex's voice, but I could no longer hear what he was saying, thankfully. However, I still *felt* the vitriol.

"Looked at from a spiritual standpoint, our discomfort in any given situation provides a signal that we are out of alignment with spiritual law and are being given an opportunity to heal something," Tipping continued.

On his way out the door for the last time, my ex ripped the headphones off my ears, got within an inch of my face, and yelled, "Yeah, *bitch*! I hope I'm the first person to ever call you that—bitch!"

And with that, he was gone. A heavy silence fell over the house. Everyone had borne witness to our messy exchange. I could *feel* their concern—and judgment. And my shame. I was humiliated. They were people I loved; they were my chosen family at the time. They were people I ate with, traveled with, learned with, and whom I cared deeply about.

As *Radical Forgiveness* continued to play against the background of my thoughts, it dawned on me that my ex actually wasn't the first person to call me a bitch. That honor belonged to my mom. I flashed back to an image of my eight-year-old self hearing my mom call me a "Black bitch" in front of my non-Black family. I realized then that I had been dating my mother. Well, not exactly, but the experience was the same, somatically and energetically.

I felt that familiar shame spread from my core throughout my entire body. I felt the sting of being publicly shamed by someone who was supposed to love and protect me. I felt the vulnerability of not being able to escape. It was the same energy that bell hooks warned us of in *All About Love*, where abuse and love seemingly coexist. This relationship embodied that concept that I had accepted as a young girl: someone who loves you can also hurt you.

As Tipping says, *"Our spiritual evolution depends heavily upon our recovery from our worst addiction—our addiction to the victim archetype, which traps us in the past and saps our life energy."*

That night, I finished the rest of the *Radical Forgiveness* audiobook and cried a different cry. It was cleansing. *I* was cleansing. That night, I committed to my healing so I would not ever have to re-perform that dynamic in that way ever again. I didn't know it then, but that was the start of my Unruly journey.

I share this moment not as an attempt to villainize my ex; or my mother, who I love dearly; or to label me as the victim. Sharing this pivotal moment is fundamental in me telling my truest story. It was clear: I was living an outdated, ill-fitting narrative. Here I was, in my twenties, still reenacting stories I had accepted as a child.

You see, I would normally have been deeply wounded by a situation like that, and at that point in my life, I had experienced many. I seemed to choose the same dynamic over and over again in different bodies. But that night, I wasn't hurt; I was empowered. The realization that I was co-creating the dynamic also meant I could *change* it. I was energized by my desperation to stop the cycle. In those moments, I bolstered a new sense of confidence in my ability to change my behavior and, therefore, my life. That moment started it all.

STOP PLAYING A PART IN YOUR LIFE AND START *BECOMING* IT

That breakup moment led me on a path of self-discovery and honesty that unleashed my personal power, and eventually led me to create the entire concept of Unruly. Being Unruly can do the same for you. The core of the Unruly Philosophy is rooted in having an honest and compassionately critical relationship with yourself. Being Unruly asks you to get curious about the role you're playing in your life. This is your story, so why not make it a true one? In order to change your story, though, you first have to get curious about it. What parts do you like? And what parts no longer work for you?

This type of investigation will require a heavy hand of compassion with yourself. We live in one of the most visible times in the history of humanity. Through social media, we have access to vast amounts of information within seconds, and we have an unprecedented view into the lives of friends, family, celebrities, and strangers. One of the consequences of this hypervisibility is that there are more opportunities for judgment and comparison, leaving us vulnerable to the effects of these opinions and judgments. Because of this, there is no better time than right now to get honest about who you are, and to perform the fullness of who you are. Being Unruly allows you to embrace the complexity of your humanity and accept the totality of who you are—but you can only do this through being truly and completely honest with yourself.

Like me, much of my community lives at an absurd intersection that always asks you to leave a part of yourself behind. Can you be a mom or a wife and still be sexy? Are you still spiritual if you run to the dance floor when you hear the opening of Juvenile's "Back That Azz Up"? Can you be Christian and have a meditation practice? Living in a black-or-white world where we're either this or that, either a mother or a carefree woman, either a wife or a sexually liberated being, is not the story for an Unruly woman. Her journey means rejecting the urge to choose a side in impossible dichotomies. Unruly women do not cherry-pick what we accept about ourselves. Being Unruly means officiating a healthy union between these seemingly contradictory parts of yourself instead of forcing yourself into a box simply because it's easier for others to digest.

Being Unruly means opening the door to those closed-off parts of yourself and having the courage to speak to the compassionate darkness. It's loving your body exactly as it is right now and still granting yourself permission to evolve it as you choose. Being Unruly means adorning your crown with your self-proclaimed terrible decisions and mistakes, providing yourself with immunity from anyone seeking to use them against you. It's setting strong boundaries that act as bridges for genuine connection instead of walls that shut everyone out. Unruly women grant themselves permission to express all their contradictions wholly and completely because this is precisely where our power lies. In learning to be completely honest with ourselves, about ourselves, and those around us, we empower ourselves to embrace who we truly are and what we truly need in life to be happy—which may be separate from what we've been taught to believe.

Unruly women are expert identity inventors, skilled communicators, adept boundary setters, proud self-celebrators, and forever compassionately curious. Unruly women are dedicated to uplifting healers and leaders who have been left out of the "zen and calm" personal growth movement. As the wellness community continues to expand and diversify, so must its thought leadership. Welcome to the side of self-help and wellness that has all the love and light, without any of the BS.

IS UNRULY FOR ME?

For those of you who may not be familiar with my work, I am the CEO and founder of Curvy, Curly, Conscious, and since 2016 we've produced retreats and events that provide safe spaces for Black women to heal and grow. I am most well known for producing The Unruly Retreat, which aims to help Black women step into their personal power through radical self-love, self-acceptance, and joy. This book is inspired by the experiences I've had at my retreats, kind of like a retreat on the page. In order to protect the integrity of my Unruly retreats, there are two questions I ask participants that need to be answered with a yes. And since this book is the physical version of an Unruly Retreat, your participation is needed here.

1. Do you identify as a Black woman?

2. Do you share the daily lived experience of a Black woman? (i.e., When you go about your day, does the world see you and treat you as a Black woman?)

I often get asked on social media and in my email why I don't open the retreat up to women of all backgrounds. After all, all women are victims of our patriarchal society. While that's true, there are certain barriers and difficulties that come with being a Black woman specifically in the north. That second question in particular aims to acknowledge those unique challenges. The issue that so many Black women have is that non-Black women feel entitled to Black spaces, even when it's clear that they are a guest. It's like that old saying "You want the rhythm but not the blues." Everyone wants to profit off of Black culture, appropriate Black culture, and be adjacent to the cool of Black culture. They want to lay their edges, wear the braids, have our curves, and tan their skin, but they don't want to show up when it's time to protest, march, organize, or disrupt the status quo. Most are also unwilling to give up any manufactured privilege and power they have inherited from their proximity to whiteness.

I could very well allow women of other backgrounds to join us on the retreat, but how could I be sure of their intentions? Are these non-Black women checking the racism they see in their families? Are they donating their time and resources to causes that will help end systemic oppression? Are they doing the internal work necessary to be anti-racist? And to be clear, dating, having sex with, or even procreating with Black people does not—and will never—absolve someone of their racism.

This sentiment reminds me of that children's story *The Little Red Hen*. The Hen was making bread for her chicks, and she asked her animal friends to help her make it, but nobody wanted to help.

"Who will help me cut the wheat?"

"Not I," responded her farm friends.

"Who will help me grind the wheat?" she asked.

"Not I," responded her farm friends.

By the end of the story, after she had single-handedly made her bread from scratch, she called her chicks to eat, and all her farm friends came, like, "Oh, can I have some bread too?"

The Hen was like, "No, no you can't. No, you can't have any of this bread that you didn't help make."

Shout-out to that Hen.

That story, while not as complicated, encapsulates the experience of Black women in so many ways. The women who are welcomed at The Unruly Retreat are tired of having to hold space for other people's opinions and experiences while minimizing their own. They're tired of doing the work to make the bread alone, only for others to come and take from their plate without putting in work themselves. One would only feel offended by not being able to come to The Unruly Retreat if they felt like they were entitled to that space in the first place. You only feel like something is taken from you if you felt like said thing belonged to you.

So, the question shouldn't even be, can non-Black people come to The Unruly Retreat? The question should be, why do non-Black people even want to come to a retreat that is meant to be a safe space for Black women? My own sister and mother cannot attend The Unruly Retreat, and they have never asked why. It makes perfect sense to them that I'm creating space for Black women, and they have never challenged me on it. And guess what? Neither can my dad or my brother. And they've never asked to attend either.

I didn't think the decision to make my retreat a safe space for Black women would be controversial, and yet, here we are.

WHAT WE'RE HERE TO LEARN

Though some may see it as controversial for Black women to gather together and uplift themselves and each other, this book isn't about them. This book is *your* Unruly experience you can take with you each day, whether you've been to one of my retreats or not. Within this book, as is the case at the in-person Unruly Retreat, we will explore what it really means to stand firmly in your inner knowing, no matter the outside circumstances, so you can begin the process of healing from old wounds, reclaiming your personal power, and stepping into it with unwavering confidence.

Throughout our lessons, I've laced in journaling prompts and exercises to guide you along your journey, inspire you to think more deeply about how you relate to the concepts, and consider how you can begin to implement them in your life right now. Together, let's create the experience of the world we desire. A world where Black women don't have to apologize for who we are, where we don't have to mold ourselves into a poorly cast role. Instead, we can mold a world to fit us. With the lessons in this book, you have the opportunity create a new experience of your world. You can tell your truest story.

Wherever you are in your personal journey when you're reading this book, it's my deepest and most genuine wish that you experience the same magic that we share at the in-person Unruly Retreat. By the end of this book, I hope you feel closer to your true essence, more connected to your higher power, and more in love with yourself than ever before.

Now, let's get Unruly.

Understand

1

The World Is Your Stage

In the summer of 2023, I hosted my first Unruly Retreat in three years. Three years might not sound like a lot of time, but this was three *pandemic* years. In that time, almost everything about my life had shifted. I'd redefined my role as a wife, started my journey to motherhood, moved to a new state, restructured my business, and, along with much of the world, experienced one of the scariest and most uncertain times of our lives in the midst of a global pandemic. I remember thinking the pandemic would be a moment of "great awakening." I thought very firmly that the collective would wake up to the ways in which late-stage capitalism and other oppressive structures have affected our mental health and quality of life. That might not have been the case overall, but for me, though, I was shaken and forced to see where I have been kept away from living all of my truth out loud.

As I began to look more critically at my daily life, I naturally began to analyze systems like capitalism, patriarchy, misogyny, and white supremacy because I feel they are intrinsically linked to our ability (or inability) to self-actualize. Self-development does not happen in a bubble. I am not completely against capitalism; if America practiced textbook capitalism, that would mean the market truly decides, and bad businesses would dissolve as the market dictates. But we live in a highly manipulated form of capitalism that has led to an extreme concentration of wealth that does not support a true democracy. Today, we are living under late-stage capitalism, also sometimes called corporate capitalism, where we no longer exchange commodities—*we* are the commodities. And on top of that, we're inundated with patriarchal and misogynistic messaging that constantly tells us we're not enough as women. Whether we realize it or not, these systems affect every single aspect of our lives, and often take a toll on our mental health.

While we may not have joined hands in collective unity during the pandemic, many people were awakened to the simple fact that they were not happy with the way their life was going and they knew they needed a change. And, in the case of my work with Black women in particular, I knew the return of The Unruly Retreat had to speak to the new world we were living in. It had to serve as a salve for the harm and chaos that we were all living through.

Since the pandemic, I, like many Americans, have felt lonelier than ever. More disconnected from myself. And because my journey to become a mother was much more difficult than I expected, I started to wonder about my overall purpose in this life. I had always wanted to be a mother ever since I worked as a nanny at thirteen years old. My clients would ask me all the time, "Who raised you? What culture are your parents from?" because I had naturally picked up domestic skills like cooking, cleaning, and nurturing so well. I always had a third sense for never sitting and always using my time, making sure the families I worked for came home to a house that was cleaner than they had left it and kids that were happy, clean, and presentable. Caring for others was an inherent skill.

I always thought being a mother would just be something that was a part of my natural progression as a woman. I never thought it would be anything I needed to think about or do anything special to achieve. So, when that didn't happen, I wondered what I would do with all this care inside of me. During this process, I started to do spiritual integration work, which is, essentially, deep shadow work. "Shadow work" is a term initially introduced by Swiss psychologist Carl Jung that refers to the parts of ourselves that we repress or disown.[1] The focus of the spiritual integration work we'll do together is on guiding you to accept everything that you're building resistance to in your life. Instead of running from the waves, you run right into them. The hope is that you can then integrate anything you're rejecting *from* yourself *into* yourself as part of your divine experience. You own every aspect of your story.

So, what that meant for me in my journey to be a mother is that I had to think about the possibility of not ever being one. This wasn't the story I had wanted, so what would I do now? Would I still feel valuable as a woman? A wife? Would I still love myself? And would I still create a life that I am in love with? Yes. I decided that I would create a life so full that even if I never birthed a child out of my body, I would be completely in love and happy with my story. Who's life was it anyway? Sure, the story was unfolding differently than I expected, but it was still *mine*.

I funneled all of that loving, caring, nurturing energy that I seek to give to my children to myself first, and then to the women of The Unruly Retreat. A mother births a child, and a child births a mother. Similarly, I created a transformative experience for Black women who, in turn, transformed me.

Because in their presence, I get to be a unique expression of the divine feminine. Consider me your Unruly Doula, guiding you through birthing the most honest, whole version of yourself that can't wait to make her entrance.

THE MORNING OF DAY 1

The morning of the retreat, I opened the balcony door to my hotel room, stepped outside, and felt the muggy air on my skin. I looked up to the gray, cloudy sky and prayed for sun. I sat in my balcony chair and gazed softly at the crisp, blue ocean before closing my eyes to begin my meditation. There's always a rush of thoughts when I first sit to meditate. I remember the words of my friend and fellow teacher, Justin Michael Williams: "If you can worry, you can meditate." Instead of fighting these thoughts off, I treat them like small children who need guidance.

"No, thank you. I see you, but not right now," I said in my mind. I took a deep breath in and focused on the sensation of the air filling my lungs and diaphragm. I held it there, feeling my heart beating and my blood pulsing through my veins. I was beginning to "drop into the meditation," as they say.

After a few rounds of breathing, I expressed my gratitude, starting with things I had a sensory connection to.

"Thank you for the sun on my skin. Thank you for my ability to breathe freely, to move freely. Thank you for my hair; I really like it today. Thank you for clean air, water, and for my coffee this morning. The coffee was really tasty."

I am going to say something you've probably heard before. Starting your meditation session with a gratitude practice is an excellent way to anchor yourself in a feeling of expansiveness and receptivity. When the average person sits down to meditate, they tend to imagine possibilities or things they wish were different. Whether it be a request for healing, forgiveness, or changed circumstances, the intention is often for a shift to happen in our lives, even if that shift is just a change in perspective. Gratitude, on the other hand, reminds us of what we already have, of the abundance we already experience, and of the prayers that have already been answered.

From a psychological perspective, gratitude can counteract some of the effects of habituation, or our inclination to get accustomed to certain situations or stimuli. It's easy to overlook something as mundane as breathing or being able-bodied, but imagine for second not being able to breathe on demand, or not being able to move parts of your body. I remember once I had a cold and I could not breathe through my nose; after I healed, I was so grateful just to breathe freely. Gratitude reminds us not to take the everyday magic around us for granted.

Gratitude also acknowledges your relationship to Spirit, or the higher power you speak to—Spirit is my word, but please feel free to substitute it with whatever word feels comfortable to you. When I pray and meditate, I use a very relatable voice and approach it like a partnership that Spirit and I are in, a partnership of ongoing co-creation as opposed to a top-down dictatorship.

From there, I moved on to the more abstract things I was grateful for.

"Thank you for trusting me to lead these women. Thank you for their trust in me. Thank you for the opportunity to raise the collective vibration." I continued to give thanks, and then I put in a request.

"Please use me. Guide me to make the decisions, to utter the words, and to provide the space that these women need. Allow us all to be the highest versions of ourselves together. Allow me to fully trust my inner guidance and this experience."

Finally, I asked myself to trust in the entirety of this experience, which included my own inner guidance. Without this, I am honestly of no use during Unruly. If I am not led by my inner guidance, then I am led by my ego and/or my fears. And simply put, the retreat is not about me. As the energetic leader, my anchor has to be the experience of the ladies and the highest good of the group. As much as I can, I stay in this intention.

YOUR MOMENT BEFORE

Fun fact: Although I don't professionally work as an actress now, it will always be a core part of who I am. I have trained as an actress since I was in my teens, even going on to get a degree from Tisch School of the Arts at NYU. My biggest takeaway from my acting studies is how much an actor's training can actually apply to their self-development journey. Above all, an actor's job is to tell the truth.

In one of my scene study classes, we were instructed to think about the circumstances that led up to a particular scene. The playwright has dominion over the words in a scene, but we, as actors, have the ability to create what's called a *moment before*. What happened *just before* this scene started, and how can you as an actor use this information to make the scene more compelling? By giving a character a moment before, you give life to them beyond what's written on the page. You enrich their story arc in the scene. The most compelling performances come from actors who have taken the time to create the moment before the action starts.

While the journey you will undertake in this book is not a stage performance, it is a *life* performance. Leaning into this process will require you to face aspects of yourself that may bring about difficult emotions, like shame, guilt, or anger. These are all normal and natural reactions, but it's important to get familiar with your moment before, your why, so you don't lose focus on the end goal.

Unruly Unquiry

Take a moment right now to get quiet and set your intention for what you'd like to gain from reading this book. Maybe you want to connect more clearly with your inner guidance, be able to listen to yourself more and accept yourself more wholly, or maybe you want to love yourself more fully.

Take a deep breath in through your nose and out through your mouth. If you'd like, you can complete this practice with your hand on your heart. Whatever you decide, let this intention be your North Star throughout this book. You deserve to realize this intention for yourself so you can be reminded of why you started this work. Answer the following questions honestly:

- Who are you right now in this moment?

- Who would you like to be by the end of this book? Describe the emotions, opportunities, and relationships you'd like to experience.

BEFORE YOU BEGIN, DROP THE JUDGMENT

There's one more thing you are going to need to do to get started: drop the judgment. Of yourself. Of others. Of God/Spirit/Universe/Insert Your Own Word. One of the overarching qualities that I'm mindful of curating at Unruly is a spirit of nonjudgmental self-observation.

I am an expert on the topic of being judgmental. As a matter of fact, you can call me Judge Judy because my inner critic was harsh! She and I have a better relationship now, but for years she ran the show, and when it was time to host my first Unruly Retreat, she affectionately came to say hi and hand me a platter of self-doubt. *What do I really have to teach these women? Am I qualified to do this? Will they like me? Will they enjoy the retreat?* Early in my Unruly journey, I absolutely would have let these questions invade my mind and corrupt my self-confidence. Now, I let them pass like clouds across a blue sky. Instead of judging myself for thinking these thoughts or entertaining them by answering those questions, I decided to be as present as possible, thank Judge Judy for her input, then ask her to leave.

JUDGMENTAL BRAIN DUMP

One of my favorite techniques for combating judgment is to do a judgmental brain dump. When I'm becoming overwhelmed by my inner critic, I set a timer for two minutes and get all those self-judgments out. Without taking my pen from the page, I let Judge Judy lay out all her accusations and critiques on a page—yes, even the ones that are absolutely ridiculous. If you find yourself in a similar mental place, I urge you to start writing, and don't stop for two minutes. The goal here is to purge all the self-doubt you can manage and leave it on the page.

After the two minutes is up, commit to letting it all go and going about your day as normal.

Being Unruly means always holding seemingly opposing truths at the same time: you are asked to be non-judgmental of yourself and others, and at the same time highly curious about yourself and your motivations. Not critical in a self-deprecating way, but as an expression of how much you love yourself. You love yourself enough to sit in truth. In the case of judgment, one of the most rewarding parts about committing to being less judgmental of yourself is that you also become less judgmental of others. You are able to access more empathy, take things less personally, and see more good in the world around you. In this way, this work is deeply personal, but also deeply connected to the world around us. No matter where you stand on the self-judgment scale, you will need to practice it in order to be Unruly. Harsh self-judgment is the quickest way to kill your progress.

- Think back to a time when you judged yourself harshly. Reflect on what happened and how your treatment of yourself impacted your ability to effectively move forward.

- Now that you clearly see your judgmental thoughts for what they are, what can you do moving forward to combat them?

AND—SCENE! THE RETREAT BEGINS

I headed down to the check-in table that my team set up right outside the hotel lobby, preparing myself to enter the soon-to-be-buzzing room on the other side of the double doors. A smile formed on my face as I heard Drake's "Blem" playing in the background. I took one last deep breath, then opened the doors to see everyone's neon swimsuits neatly laid out on the welcome table, with our white Unruly logo displayed. I browsed the name tags, and the realization hit me that each one represented a real-life human being who had agreed to take this journey with me. I've even prepared a name tag for you so you can relish in the excitement as well: Unruly [insert your name here].

The first bus pulled up and out poured a group of women with the energy of excited kids arriving at summer camp. Spilling out of the van, they squealed and laughed and hugged each other with yoga mats in hand. I ran up to greet them and started checking folks in, handing out name tags, and taking selfies. The retreat had officially begun.

And your retreat on a page has officially begun as well. Take a moment on your own to channel the emotions you may be feeling in this moment, whether you are excited to meet your future self or you're nervous for the journey ahead. All feelings are valid here.

If you have a phone nearby, snap a selfie to commemorate the start of your own personal retreat.

Repeat after me: I am open and willing to become the woman of my dreams.

2

Setting the Scene for Safety

At The Unruly Retreat, the welcome orientation is where I get the group on the same emotional and spiritual footing. There can't be a group transformation without setting this foundation. The ladies are all coming from different places, experiences, mindsets, beliefs, ideas, etc.—and so are you. What you need to prepare for the experience ahead will be different from what I need or what another reader may need. So while you meditate, pray, express gratitude, and set intentions and goals, be honest about where you are on the journey right now and try not to compare your circumstances to where someone else may be or where you think you "should" be.

This book is your safe space to begin the process of deconstructing your identities, which can be scary. This is the whole reason why ladies come to The Unruly Retreat, and it's likely why you're reading this book. You want to experience emotional, physical, and spiritual safety, which is a healing tonic in itself. Your nervous system is connected by what psychology calls the vagus nerve, but I like to use Resmaa Menakem's term "the soul nerve" because, as Menakem states, it's a "much stickier and more descriptive term."[1]

Our soul nerve tells us when we are safe and when we are in danger. Although for the most part, this process does not happen consciously, many of us spend our lives in fight-or-flight mode, awaiting a potential threat. When we actively seek calm and peace, we are able to heal our emotional body and retrain our nervous system to the experience of safety. The book in your hands is a sacred space for you to freely and deeply explore yourself. It's okay to be vulnerable here. Allow your future, freer, safer self to guide you. Surrender to her leading this process and allow her to be in the driver's seat from here on out.

- Take a moment to think about how you feel right now. Are you feeling excited? Optimistic? Nervous? Apathetic? Why do you think you are feeling this way?

- Who could you be if you could be completely safe? What version of yourself could live in complete safety? Take a moment to describe this version of yourself.

From my acting training, I learned that one of the best ways to develop group cohesion and dissolve nervous energy is through an active warm up—so in dramatic, theatrical, Unruly fashion, that's exactly what we're going to do! But first, it's important that we understand the impact our thoughts can have on the process.

Stepping onto the stage for the first time in front of the group reminded me of the rush I'd get right before I went out in front of an audience during my theater days. I remember looking out into the audience at the retreat and seeing everyone's smiling faces and apprehension. I could practically feel the questions in the air: *Am I going to make friends? Am I going to be accepted? Are they going to like me? Am I going to enjoy myself? Is this woo-woo stuff really gonna work? Can I really change? How will I do this journey alone?*

You may have similar questions floating through your head right now, and I don't blame you. But if there's one thing I've learned from my acting training, it's that sometimes you have to get out of your head and into your body. Healing does not only occur through the logical mind; it can, but not exclusively. I've found that healing through the logical mind alone can be limiting, as some of our experiences are not processed logically in our body. Trauma is not processed rationally, and healing can be unpredictable. Sometimes we are reliving old stories in the present that might feel true but are actually us performing a version of ourselves that's connected to previous trauma. Tapping into our somatic experience, in addition to logical processing, allows us to be present with what feelings and sensations we are actually experiencing *right now*. Being Unruly requires a level of freedom that can only be accessed by imagining, dreaming, and believing beyond the bounds of logic. The safe container that I create allows this type of playfulness to thrive. Play is a core part of my healing approach. Life is hard enough; healing shouldn't always feel like another task on your to-do list.

THE SPECTRUM GAME

"We're going to play what I call The Spectrum Game," I informed the ladies at the retreat. "Imagine there is a diagonal line going across the entire room, starting from this corner, 'Hell Yes'—" I motioned to the back left corner of the room, "—all the way to the top right corner, 'Hell No,'" I motioned to the other corner. "I'm going to ask a question, and you're going to give your answer by standing somewhere along this spectrum. For example, if your answer is 'Hell No,' you'll stand all the way in the top right corner; if your answer is 'Hell Yes,' you'll stand all the way in the back left corner; and if your answer is 'Maybe,' you'll stand somewhere in the middle. It's your job to place yourself along the spectrum, based on your answer."

The hushed murmurs and nodding clued me in that everyone understood, so I began to give prompts:

"I am happy to be at The Unruly Retreat." The room scattered to the back left corner of the room.

"This is my first ever Unruly Retreat." A group of women moved from that crowded back left corner to the top right "Hell No" corner.

"I am here solo." There was movement around the room, but the majority of the women stayed in the "Hell Yes" corner.

"Notice I said 'solo' and not 'alone.' You may have come solo, but you are never alone in your journey to befriend your truest self," I said. Smiles crept across everyone's faces as they exchanged glances of understanding and excitement. I actually recommend ladies come to The Unruly Retreat solo because when you come by yourself, you're more likely to be open-minded, meet new people, and step outside of your comfort zone. The same goes for you, Unruly Reader. If you've embarked on this journey of emotional growth and self-care solo, then you, too, may be more likely to step outside of your comfort zone without fear of judgment from others; and if you're reading this as part of a group, then be sure to encourage each other so you, too, can find a deeper sisterhood in this process.

"I am invested in my healing journey," I continued. The entire group came back to the "Hell Yes" corner. I was extremely happy to see this because this is what sets Unruly apart from being a vacation, and this is what sets this book apart from being just another self-growth book. The Unruly journey works by combining fun and joy with self-work and collective healing.

"I am living my truest story."

Women moved about the space, but most people floated in the "Maybe" area. This statement is the core of the Unruly Philosophy (more on this later).

"Turn to the person next to you and tell them what you think that sentence means," I instructed. I walked around the room, eavesdropping on conversations and checking the room temperature. I overheard different answers throughout my walk around the room: "Not letting anyone define who you are." "Having healthy boundaries." "Being honest." "Keeping your cup full." "Accepting yourself 100 percent."

Unruly Inquiry

If you are able, you can do this exercise just like we did, actually placing yourself physically along a diagonal line in your room. If you're not in a space to move around, you can place an X on the lines below for the following prompts, according to where your answer is on the spectrum of Hell Yes to Hell No.

"I am invested in my healing journey."

    Hell Yes _____ Hell No

"I am open to reevaluating my perspective about myself."

    Hell Yes _____ Hell No

"I believe in my ability to grow."

    Hell Yes _____ Hell No

"I am living my truest story."

    Hell Yes _____ Hell No

How do you feel about where your answers are oriented on the spectrum?

_____

_____

_____

Which answers would you like to lean more toward Yes or No?

_____

_____

_____

    Take a moment to sit with how you would feel if you were living your *truest* story.

I could sense that Mission: Break the Ice had been a success with The Spectrum Game. I could visibly see the difference in the room. Shoulders were more relaxed. There were fewer visible nervous tics on display, like feet and hand tapping. The women looked more familiar with each other and less formal. And I hope you feel that way too. So, with that, let's talk about The Crooked Room.

THE CROOKED ROOM

Imagine you are standing in an empty room with just a chair in it. You walk toward the chair and immediately notice that your balance is askew. You maneuver your way to the chair and attempt to sit, but your body slides to one side of the chair. As hard as you try you cannot stand up straight in this room. After a while, you look down at the floor and it dawns on you: the chair is crooked. Not only that, the entire room is crooked.

In *Sister Citizen: Shame, Stereotypes, and Black Women in America*, author Melissa V. Harris-Perry describes a field dependence study that shows how people find orientation in space. In the study, subjects were put into a crooked room with a crooked chair and were asked to align themselves vertically. The study found that people could be tilted by as much as 35 degrees and still report that they were standing perfectly straight because they determined their alignment based on the tilted images.[2] Some participants thought they were standing completely upright because they had adjusted themselves to the crookedness of the room. There was nothing wrong with their ability to stand up straight; they were standing in a crooked room.

As you probably already noticed, throughout this book I'm going to be making departures from self-investigation to comment on larger structures that I believe contribute to one's ability or inability to self-actualize. Structures including, but not limited to, capitalism, misogyny, and white supremacy. I really wish that I could just write a book that didn't have to comment on any of these topics, but it would be spiritually disingenuous for me to do so. I would not be being honest. I believe that these systems directly impact one's ability to create the life that they desire, and not commenting on that is not being truthful, and actually harmful. Because it ignores the context in which the circumstances of your life were created. We might not live in a more equitable, humane, just world that honors us, but we do what we can to improve our lives in the meantime. As much as I want the revolution to occur (whether it's televised or not), in the meantime, we can be Unruly.

And this is why the aim here is not to "fix you." You do not need fixing. You are here to be *unfixed*. There's nothing wrong with your legs; you're just not on solid ground. Judging yourself for being off-balance on an uneven surface neglects the circumstances that create your loss of balance. It would be even worse to compare yourself to someone standing on a flat surface.

You were born into a crooked room, a room where you as a Black woman are not often seen, heard, or even acknowledged. The inability to stand up straight and perform to society's expectations is not solely a personal flaw; it could also point to the imperfection of the room. If you're struggling with mental health issues like depression, anxiety, low self-worth, or imposter syndrome, I would argue that could be a natural consequence of living in a deeply troubled society. What if your brain is responding exactly how it's meant to? What if your brain is doing the best it can to adapt to the Crooked Room?

Hear me clearly. This is 100 percent not absolving you of taking responsibility for your own actions in life. This is not a hall pass for you to evade personal accountability for your actions, thoughts, and beliefs. There is absolutely no way you will move toward a more evolved, healed version of yourself without taking inventory of how you are showing up at any given moment. However, historically, there has been an overemphasis on policing Black bodies, and Black behavior, especially Black women's behavior. Social media is inundated with posts urging Black women to take accountability for their wrongdoings in the family structure and in the Black community as a whole, but we don't seem to ever move past that part. If I go on YouTube right now and tune in to any popular conversations about Black love and relationships, I am going to immediately hear "think pieces" about how women are afraid to take accountability, and I personally think that's bullshit—Grade A, USDA bullshit.

On the contrary, women are often the first to take accountability, whether it's privately or publicly. We are quite literally trained and conditioned to do so. Because we live in a patriarchal society, which by definition places more value on men than women, we've historically been targeted as scapegoats for society's ills. Between the fifteenth and eighteenth centuries when men feared losing religious control, women were the first to be persecuted as witches. In the nineteenth century, women's serious mental health issues were dismissed as *hysteria*, or a women's inability to control her emotions. And Eve is still blamed today for eating the apple and desecrating the Garden of Eden in the Christian church.

Blaming women for others' fears or bad behavior is an ugly byproduct of Western patriarchy, so much so that we are mentally and emotionally trained by society to take accountability for *other* people's actions. We take them on as our own. We apologize for our partners' behavior. We assume full responsibility for our children's outcomes. Sometimes, we even take responsibility for our entire family, serving as the easy scapegoat for cracks in the family system. From what I see, we are constantly looking for ways in which we can take *more* accountability, and as a result, women are more likely to receive mental health treatment and are overrepresented in the self-help space. Collectively, we are used to investigating our part in a given issue, so in the pages of this book, no, I will not be overemphasizing accountability and "fixing" your problems. I think we have had enough of that.

The simple fact that you've picked up this book means you are already engaging in the practice of self-accountability. What I would argue is that you don't have enough compassion for yourself just yet. You're probably fluent in taking account of how your actions lead to certain outcomes in your life, but you have yet to express the fullness of who you are or tell your complete story.

It's nearly impossible to develop an intimate, loving, and accepting relationship with yourself while living with that kind of harshness. If your relationship with yourself starts and ends at accountability, what's next? In order to really get to know ourselves, we need to do so in a kind way. Otherwise, we get overwhelmed and risk stopping our journey of healing and understanding completely. Hyper-focusing on accountability can bring us to a point of self-blame, and at worst, encourage victim-blaming. And there's already so much evidence in popular culture to support the idea that it's all your fault, that you just aren't doing enough, that you just need to do this one more thing, that we sometimes never get to the self-love part. This is especially true for Black women who, whether consciously or unconsciously, seek to live beyond the lazy or "angry Black woman" stereotypes placed on them. But a lack of self-compassion prevents us from ever experiencing true self-love. We become jagged in our thoughts about ourselves, and we use that mindset as a weapon against ourselves, disconnecting us from our potential for deep mental, emotional, and spiritual growth. Every time I remind a Black woman that part of her experience is a symptom of larger social structures, it relieves some of the pressure. She is reminded that her slouching is partly due to the world being askew.

For most of my life, one of the biggest criticisms I've received is that I'm "too sensitive and too emotional." Across TV, movies, and in our interpersonal lives, Black women are celebrated for being strong and for *not* showing emotion. But are these women strong, or are they just really good at repressing their feelings? Are these women strong, or are they experts at disconnecting from themselves? Are they strong, or are they engaging in survival tactics to get through everyday life? I'm tired of seeing women crouch to adjust to the Crooked Room. I'm tired of seeing women make themselves smaller to be accepted. I'm tired of seeing women with such empathy, such softness, such sensitivity turn themselves hard just to survive. So many women want to be soft; they want to put the metaphorical boxing gloves down and—as podcast bros love to suggest—rest in their femininity. The desire is there, but there's no safe foundation for it. Many women have divorced themselves from what they actually want and what feels most true to them as a means of protection. They are performing someone else's story entirely.

ADJUSTING YOUR POSTURE IN THE CROOKED ROOM

I absolutely acknowledge that I have a very specific entry point when it comes to race, being raised as the only Black person in my household. I have a hyper-awareness around race, which I would argue many Black bodies have developed as a survival skill. Whenever I hear someone ask, "Why does everything have to be about race?" it tells me a lot about who they are and what they haven't had to endure. As Justin Michael Williams and Shelly Tygielski put it, "Privilege isn't about what you've gone through, it's about what you *haven't* gone through."[3] To even ask that question suggests that you have a certain power and privilege to even imagine a world where race *doesn't* play a factor in how you live your life. I'm not sure I've *ever* had an experience that *wasn't* informed by race in some capacity.

For example, to this day, I still don't feel completely safe around non-Black "bodied" people, a term used in Resmaa Menakem's book *My Grandmother's Hands* that speaks to how racial trauma manifests in the body.[4] I notice when I'm around white-bodied people, I find myself focused on being on my best behavior, which I then judge about myself. I dislike this tendency in myself, but this impulse is not mine alone. There is a long history of violence and harm on Black bodies who have dared to make white people uncomfortable. My body has this remembrance of minding my p's and q's around white people, and, in protecting myself, it's as if I get this internal silent alarm signal that reminds me I'm not all the way safe in their presence. It's these encounters that are in my mind when someone says: "Why does everything have to be about race?"

And if we're being honest, what *isn't* about race? There wouldn't even be a United States of America without racism. The forced labor of almost 10 million enslaved Africans during the Transatlantic Slave Trade funded the development of the New World and other countries across the globe, like Brazil, Cuba, the Caribbean, Germany, and beyond.[5] We exist in the shadows of this history as our racial trauma haunts us through microaggressions, code switching, and that uneasy feeling I get in my body around non-Black folks. It's this stifling Crooked Room that Unruly women desire to break free from. They want a break from having to translate their own experience to other people, or teaching people about racism, or explaining why something is harmful or hurtful, or being told that something isn't that bad, or that they're not really seeing what they're seeing. It's exhausting. It's a grinding everyday experience to have to fight for your own humanity.

The truth is we're *all* in this Crooked Room together. Our individual rooms may look a little different, but they are all built with the same materials. I would also argue that we all share a larger Crooked Room (ex. living in America, living under capitalism, being a woman, etc.), but this book is not necessarily about mending those larger structures. Instead, our focus is on our individual experiences and the elements we can control within the dysfunction that surrounds us. In order to deconstruct our personal Crooked Rooms, we need to first describe what's in the room. Inside your Crooked Room sits all the messaging that asks you to go against yourself, all the limiting beliefs that hold you back from your ability to self-actualize and step into your authenticity. Inside your Crooked Room might be messaging like: you are only valuable when you have proximity to a man, your value is inextricably linked to the material possessions you have access to, or your worth is directly correlated to a particular beauty standard. What direct or indirect ideas conflict with your most honest self?

Tune in to your body to feel when something is off or like a betrayal to your true self. For example, you may:

- Feel hot all of a sudden

- Experience an increased heart rate

- Find it harder to breathe normally

- Feel the need to over-rationalize why you should go along with something

- Experience a sense of overall discomfort in your body when you think about this topic

Unruly Unquiry

- What societal messages have you accepted in your life that ask you to go against how you actually feel about yourself? Examples: "I should be more successful by now. I am not worthy of love. I am not good at relationships. People that love me also leave me. There's something intrinsically wrong with me."

- How do the people you call family make you feel about yourself? Examples: "I should be married by a certain age. I should have kids by a certain age. I should have chosen a different career path. I am not a good daughter/sister/cousin/etc. I should be doing more for my family. I stand out too much."

- How does your community make you feel about yourself? Examples: "It's hard to make new friends. People do not want the best for me. Good friends are hard to come by. I can't trust people. I don't fit in. It's hard to be accepted by others. I am better off alone."

- How do certain systems, like religious institutions, educational institutions, etc., make you feel about yourself? Examples: "The government/school/bank/job/place of worship doesn't genuinely care about my well-being. I can't trust them."

The good news is you are the only one who can change *your* life—and you are in the right place for that. What I have to offer you is genuine compassion, care, concern, and proven strategies that have worked for me and the women that I love.

The notion that you need fixing rests on you thinking you're not good enough as you are. If you accept that premise, how will you know when you've reached your goal? What signifiers or markers will be present to tell you when you're good enough?

Fuck that. Respectfully. There's a way to work toward a more evolved version of yourself without accepting that something is *wrong* with you. No, you are simply adjusting your posture in this Crooked Room. You are evolving and growing, and at the same time absolutely perfect as you are right now.

How can you really ever get to the bottom of who you are and why you are without examining the larger structures that have contributed to your development? This is something that is missing from a lot of self-development ideology that seems to exist in an apolitical, aracial, ahistorical place, where you can literally do anything, manifest anything, and be anything simply by adjusting your thoughts, perspective, or vibration. This is completely out of context of political, racial, and historical influences on Black, Brown, and Indigenous people around the world, especially us as Black women.

Now, I do believe you can adjust your third-dimensional reality and change your life by reprogramming your thoughts, beliefs, actions, and vibrations. I do it in my life all the time, and I've seen miracles happen for others in the face of belief, faith, and work. However, many women do not have the privilege of seeing a world that is not colored by race, gender, and economic policy. Even when I am in a room of my peers—highly educated, hard-working, curious, thoughtful women—more than half the room will comment on their inability to earn an appropriate wage for their expertise and talent and how that affects their self-esteem. Crooked Room.

It's disingenuous to tell marginalized people that all they need to do is pull themselves up by their bootstraps and "fix their mindset," otherwise their situation is completely their fault. Crooked Room. Never mind any of the historical circumstances that led up to those thoughts, behaviors, and actions. Crooked Room.

So, throughout the book, I want you to keep the Crooked Room in mind. Can you hold two seemingly opposing truths at the same time? Can you move toward a higher version of yourself while also accepting and loving the version of you that exists right now? Can you hold the weight of knowing that you are affected by circumstances outside of yourself and, at the same time, be serious and dedicated to how you personally show up in this world? Of course you can! Things are always, all the time, happening to us from the outside and the inside, and there's a relationship between outside stimuli and how we process it internally. We're all doing the best we can in this Crooked Room, and instead of constantly adjusting ourselves to fit a sick world, we should become more invested in creating a safe space to just *be*.

I think people hesitate to acknowledge the ways oppressive systems affect their everyday life because they see it as "giving up" their individual power or failing to take personal responsibility. But I see the exact opposite. Recognizing that you are okay exactly how you are right now actually paves the way for deep change.

It's important I set the tone in this way because I want to ensure that you are clear about the framework we'll be working in. Open your mind to doing this mental and emotional work from a place of already being okay where you are. Sometimes the place where you belong will not exist until you create it, until you understand what truly matters—living the life you've always wanted; tapping into that memory that lives within your body, mind, and spirit; and being open and honest.

My most genuine hope for you is that you can stand firmly in your inner knowing, no matter the outside circumstances that your life or society imposes on you. I hope this book frees you from crouching, tucking, or hunching to adjust to this Crooked Room.

Unruly Inquiry

Take a moment to describe the version of yourself you want to birth through this Unruly process. Write about this dream version of yourself with as much detail as possible.

Take note of any hesitancy you may feel to dream out loud.

For extra credit, you can record what you wrote as a voice note and play it back to yourself or use it in meditation. Notice what happens in your body when you hear those words.

Repeat after me: I am ready to stand tall and embrace the fullness of who I am.

Unconfirmed

3

Becoming Unbecoming

Having a group of almost one hundred beautiful Black women prancing about a resort with matching totes and swimwear, giving off all the good vibes—we definitely get a lot of attention. We always garner a lot of curious onlookers. One of the ladies told me that she was on the elevator with her Unruly tote bag, and a middle-aged white man asked her why she was at a retreat called "Unruly"?

"Unruly? That doesn't sound like a good thing. That's not very becoming," he said.

Welp, he's definitely not my target market, because over here, being unbecoming means you're doing it right. What he was implying was, why didn't she want to be a well-behaved woman? Why didn't she want to conform to respectability politics that ultimately are there to serve men's comfortability? Why didn't she want to be reserved, quiet, polite, and overly concerned with her social standing as a *good* woman? Historically, the definitions of what makes a *good* woman are arbitrary—not too talkative, non-confrontational, career-driven (but not too much), relationship-focused (but not too much), a caregiver, having a thin body frame. These standards were created from a patriarchal mindset, which doesn't see women as fully human, so by subscribing to these standards faithfully, many women find they must trade in parts of their humanity to meet them. Women are generally expected to perform a very narrow version of womanhood, and anything that doesn't fit the prescribed standards at the time are considered "unladylike" or "unbecoming."

Being Unruly is about orienting yourself back to yourself. Again, being Unruly is living your most authentic story. It's important to be aware of societal norms (most of which are manifestations of the Crooked Room) so you can decide which ones you want to subscribe to and which you don't, but you should have that choice. Being a well-behaved woman typically serves the interest of others at the expense of yourself, leading to people-pleasing behaviors that over time make us manipulative, passive-aggressive, and out of touch with our needs. I've worked with many women who were conditioned to be people pleasers, always considering the experience of others before their own, only to be left feeling silenced and resentful as an adult. Self-empowerment comes when you're able to unplug from the matrix of these respectability politics or the idea that only women who behave in "acceptable" ways are deserving of humanity. Being empowered is embracing all the dynamic aspects of yourself and wholly honoring your inner diversity (more on this later). Empowerment looks like refusing to reject any part of yourself, using both your strengths and perceived weaknesses to align with your highest good. Contrary to mainstream ideas about empowerment, while being empowered is a magnificent experience for a woman, the journey there can be unexpected.

When I decided to leave my unhealthy relationship, I was terrified. I had told everyone we were getting married, and I had invested my time, money, and energy into this relationship, allowing it to be a marker of my success and achievement. When I left, I was broken and hopeless, but at least I had me. I had refused to sacrifice myself to be in proximity to a man. At the time, I felt like I had nothing, but I really had *everything*. I had my ability to dream, to heal, and to create a new reality for myself. I empowered myself to birth a new Shelah who ultimately became the woman writing this book.

Self-empowerment is so important to me because I'm tired of seeing my sisters dismissing brilliant and exciting aspects of who they are because that's not how they think they should be. The way society teaches women to flatten themselves, shrink themselves, quiet their brilliance, and hide their uniqueness for the sake of being more palatable, frankly, pisses me off.

I have clumsily worked my way through ideas around women's liberation throughout my life without even knowing it. I have embodied different aspects of myself at different times. I've failed out loud and in private. It excites me when I see bold women living out loud, driven by their desire for liberation. There is liberation in becoming unbecoming. I have seen women say "F you" to the patriarchy and other oppressive structures, but that in itself isn't necessarily empowering. Your power isn't in running from what you don't want—it's in going toward exactly what you do want.

I want you to be able to have a life where no part of you will be left behind. Whether you desire to be a mother *and* sexy, be spiritual *and* turn up, or be a business mogul *and* well rested, you shouldn't have to choose only one option exclusively, forever. You don't have to operate as one aspect of yourself forever, and you certainly don't have to "pick a side" to live a successful life.

In some ways, we are living our mothers' and grandmothers' wildest dreams. Without knowing it, I have been embodying the Unruly Philosophy my whole life. The unique circumstances of my youth have prompted this strong sense of curiosity, where I am consistently redefining and discovering new parts of myself. Throughout my life, I have been an actress, a director, a teacher, a student, a writer, a wife, and right now, I am evolving into the next phase of myself. This ability to freely change gives me a deep sense of power and freedom that no one can take away from me. No failure or setback is greater than my ability to evolve. A powerful shift in focus occurs when you commit to following your internal guidance, no matter how unbecoming it may look.

A great example of this is after I went through several miscarriages. For a while, I had accepted that being a mother was a requirement for me to be a good wife and a "whole" woman. Accepting that fact would require me to be a slave to that desire, resting my sense of self on my journey to be a mom. Instead, I decided to use that moment as an opportunity to discover a new part of myself. What else is there for me to learn through the experience? Who else do I have a chance to be? This self-reflection, this desire to step into my fullness as a human being, is ultimately what led me to develop the Unruly Philosophy:

A **whole** and **compassionate acceptance** of your **inner diversity**.

WHOLE

The word "whole" signifies an all-encompassing, undivided acceptance that does not have any stipulations. To be Unruly is to wholly accept every aspect of your behavior, thoughts, actions, and life experience—not just the parts you perceive as good or socially acceptable. This might mean accepting the part of yourself that hates household chores, forgets to put things in her Google calendar, lets her kids eat junk food, begrudgingly goes to church once a month, and sometimes overbooks herself. Make peace with the version of you who skips workouts, misses meditation sessions, and doesn't always stick to her New Year's resolutions. The version of you who made those choices, whatever they may be, is still valid, useful, and intelligent.

COMPASSIONATE

It's a tall order to practice self-acceptance, and I am by no means saying it's easy. This is why Unruly women need a healthy dose of compassion, or the ability to be gentle and understanding, in order to move through the work it takes to accept themselves wholly. Compassion will serve as your fuel to keep going when mishaps occur. Compassion provides the kindness and empathy that you'll need to keep a soft heart even in hard times. Without compassion, the journey can become too arduous, and we may feel pressured to give up altogether. Compassion makes the acceptance possible (more on this in chapter 5). For example, after what I considered to be a failed relationship, I had the urge to harshly scold myself so I wouldn't make the same mistake again. But all that really did was make me feel even worse about myself, which made me feel stuck and uninspired. But when I was able to show myself some grace, accept the situation for what it was, and tap into my compassionate spirit, I felt lighter, more optimistic, and more inspired to change my circumstances.

INNER DIVERSITY

Take a moment to think about anything in your life that the world would consider unbecoming, unladylike, or unwanted. I want you to consider the thought that you can never reach a sense of wholeness and truth without integrating those parts into your identity. When you push away unwanted aspects that are actually a part of your life's experience, you create a watered-down performance of yourself that is ultimately a lie. We all have inner diversity, but too few of us capitalize on it. We can't do that if we're rejecting it. If I would have listened to people telling me I am too sensitive, you wouldn't be reading this book right now. Open yourself to the possibility of being a complex, complicated woman who's always in flow, and at all times moving toward the most honest version of herself.

Unruly Inquiry

Whole

- On a scale of 1 to 10, how wholly do you currently accept all aspects of yourself?

- What aspects of yourself do you have trouble accepting? Why do you think this is the case?

Compassion

- On a scale of 1 to 10, how compassionate are you with yourself?

- How can you show yourself more compassion in your everyday life?

Inner Diversity

- On a scale of 1 to 10, how much do you currently honor your inner diversity?

- What contradictions do you embody within yourself?

COMMON QUESTIONS

When I first introduce the Unruly Philosophy to retreat participants and propose a way for women to start this journey with me, I often get a lot of similar questions from each group. You may be pondering these same questions, so let's dive into them now so we can pave a clear path forward without any hesitation.

How do I become Unruly?

You don't *become* Unruly, you *uncover* it. Being Unruly is the process of unbecoming that which no longer serves you and becoming the actor, writer, and director of your own story. You are already all the things you have yet to discover within you, they just need to be given the right platform and the proper context to express themselves. This is not about changing who you are or becoming a different person, this is about honoring all of your eccentricities and complexities and being honest about who you are, flaws and all. It's about trusting yourself enough to potentially go against how society, family, and other governing structures say you should act.

How do I know when I am doing it right?

Only you can answer this question because I am not offering up an objective right or wrong. What is right for you may not work for others. Instead, I would advise you to reject dichotomous thinking altogether because it requires you to choose, and choosing implies you leave behind parts of yourself, which is opposite of this process of reclamation. Lean into how you feel and what makes you feel at peace within yourself. A better question is "Am I being true?"

What if my partner/friend/family doesn't support me on this journey?

First of all, my heart goes out to you, because it's crushing not to be supported by the people who matter most to you. This is unfortunately a painful yet unavoidable part of your growth journey. You are bound to encounter someone in your life who doesn't understand or agree with your choices. When this happens, be intentional about not taking in their critiques wholly. Instead, treat their feedback like a buffet. Look at their comments objectively, see what's there, and only take what serves you. People's opinions about your life are, ironically, rarely about you, and many times they say more about their inflexibility than anything else. At the same time, if you are offended or hurt by any of their feedback, take note of what it is exactly that offends or hurts you, as this can indicate an emotional wound you may have regarding this aspect. On the flip side, I have noticed that many Unruly women do experience relationship friction at the beginning of their journey but end up with deeper, more meaningful connections in the long run.

Who can I look to? I don't have a model for this.
Many of us do not have models to follow when creating a new path, and this can indeed be framed as a setback, but it also can be an opening for an even deeper level of freedom. You get to create your own model for how you want to live your life. You are the guru, the expert, the teacher you've been looking for. Trust what you think, feel, and believe, especially when it concerns your personal growth and self-accountability. With that said, it can still be helpful to have models to look up to, and if that is something you need along the way, feel free to get creative with finding inspiration.

First, in your journal, decide which qualities you'd like your teachers or guides to embody, then do a little research to find folks who embody those qualities. You can look to religious texts, literature, film/TV, or other women in your life or community who resonate with you. When you find those people, jot down a few notes about how they embody the qualities you look up to.

Now, you're going to do an Uno Reverse. Consider that everything you wrote about that person applies to you. Read what you wrote again, and this time, hear these words about *you*. Consider that what you admire in others is already in you. Now, list the ways in which you already have those qualities that you initially cited in someone else. What evidence do you have to support this new discovery?

If you want to take this a step further, you can meditate on the woman you admire. You can request her to guide you, or you can simply spend time with her energetically in a meditation.

The Unruly Philosophy is meant to be your North Star as you navigate these lifestyle changes and perspective shifts. Of course, I don't expect you to get it 100 percent right immediately, and you shouldn't expect that of yourself either. The whole point of this journey is that you face some hard truths and learn more about yourself as you step into your courage. Take your time learning about and accepting who you are, and if you're having trouble liking that reflection in the mirror, the next chapter can help you see yourself in a different light.

Repeat after me: I compassionately embrace the totality of my inner diversity.

4

Main Character Energy

For many years, I felt the need to make my entire home spotless before having company, for fear of judgment for not having a tidy house. No matter how many times my friends told me they didn't care, you would still find me scrubbing and shining my house prior to having guests. Over time I've learned that this impulse can be isolating, because is a home *ever* clean enough? Oh, there's laundry to be put away, I don't have any food prepared, or there are Amazon boxes in the kitchen. I brought this up to some friends casually at dinner one night and it turns out we were all doing the same thing, separately. Here we were meeting at a restaurant because we didn't feel our own spaces were acceptable enough—and when we really get down to it, the people who love you don't care. If you only let people in when your space is pristine and perfect, you'll miss out on many opportunities for deep connection and community. This is also the case for you. This chapter is about stepping up to claim your mess and releasing any shame or rejection of it, so you can connect more freely and deeply with yourself and others.

You don't have to clean up before company, metaphorically speaking. That is a fallacy that will keep you isolated and living a lie.

For the moment, leave everything where it is. Don't touch a thing. Let your journey be born from how much you love and accept who you are now and *not* from a place of how much you want to change yourself. I promise you will naturally evolve throughout this journey—but ironically, I don't want that to be your goal. You are not running from yourself or trying to escape yourself; instead, this work should be inspired by knowing how you deserve to live your own life regardless of your perceived flaws.

The mistakes. The people you had no business dating. The missed opportunities. The times where you put your foot in your mouth. That's your mess. It's also what's standing in the way of you living truthfully. Here, I offer you the opportunity to reclaim the word "mess." Mess = any self-described unwanted experiences, behaviors, or emotions. Your mess is your power. It is the sum of your perceived mistakes—but notice I said *perceived* mistakes, meaning they're not truly failures or areas that require your guilt or shame. The shame and guilt come from accepting a story you've created *about* the mess, but not necessarily from the mess itself. All of these mess-ups were needed for you to be exactly who and where you are right now, and if you can agree to creating a new story, you'll no longer need to experience those unwanted feelings like guilt or shame about your mess.

The way you flip the script on your mess is by owning it fully and completely, without judgment. If mess happened to you, if you had to endure it, you also deserve to benefit from it—but you can only benefit from mess you've reclaimed. This type of reclamation is the essence of Main Character Energy (MCE). Main Character Energy is about owning everything about who you are, in the spotlight—not in the shadows. Main Character Energy is not about feeding your ego from a place of lack. Ego-driven behavior where you think everything is about you is not honest and not conducive to being in community with others. In reality, what goes on in other people's stories is almost never about you. In my example about cleaning, I was allowing my mess to come in the way of what I really wanted (to connect with friends) because I had invented a story on behalf of other people (thinking my friends would judge me). The truth is, we were all having a similar experience, and if we would have been able to be truthful about that, we would *all* have felt less shame and guilt about it.

MCE frees you so that you no longer feel the need to heavily center yourself in other people's stories. The need to act within the story of someone else is a sign that you're not playing a big enough role in your own. You're the main character in your story, they are the main in theirs. A hallmark of ego-driven behavior is that it's comparative and points away from the self. Ego says, "My house is clean; therefore, I am a better wife/mother than you." It says, "I make six figures, so I am more hardworking than you. Look at my car, my house, and all of these markers of success." You see how the attention has been directed outside? Ego is inherently referential. MCE, on the other hand, redirects you to focus on how *you* feel about the state of your own life. Do *you* feel like a good partner? Do *you* acknowledge the effort it takes to keep a busy home clean? Why are you so concerned about a clean home? Is it coming from a place of genuine care or are you trying to prove something to someone else? Likewise, do you feel successful? Do *you* give yourself the proper acknowledgment that you need when you complete major accomplishments? Are you driven by your own internal compass or by a need for outer validation? The main goal of embodying MCE is for you to have the courage to take inventory of your mess and then decide what you actually want for yourself moving forward.

MAIN CHARACTER ENERGY

I spent decades of my life trying to avoid the Main Character spotlight, for fear of people critiquing my eccentricities. For years, I would twist and tilt my body to orient myself to this Crooked Room. I would hide my love of nerdy things—like quantum physics, astronomy, and film theory—just to be accepted. By doing this, I was acting as a supporting character in my own life. It wasn't until my thirties that I began reclaiming my mess and decided to stand up straight without first considering the angle of the room. I became the Main Character in my story by diving into the methods I will share with you here. I love it here. I think you will too.

Main Character Energy is reclaiming all the *shouldas*—"I shoulda done this. They shoulda done that. I shoulda known better. I shoulda done this by now." Living in the past and lamenting about how you could have acted differently is like trying to climb a mountain with an anchor on your foot. It'll just weigh you down. There's a difference between taking accountability—which is a healthy process of taking inventory of your actions—and shame, which only functions to make you feel bad. Stepping into your Main Character Energy is about making peace with your mess and allowing it to become your strength so no one can use it against you, not even yourself. Your flaws become adornments to your crown, and those life experiences you wish you could erase become the bright spots in the mosaic that is you. Sit down at the table with the materials you've been given and grant yourself permission to create a masterpiece.

Main Character Energy encapsulates the rebelliousness associated with being Unruly. It is rejecting the pressure to flatten yourself out, to pick a side, or to fit yourself into a preconceived mold. In order to fully claim the spotlight in your own story, you're gonna have to get okay with being called contradictory or a hypocrite. We are taught that changing your mind could mean you're untrustworthy; that taking a new path could mean you're disingenuous; that learning, growing, and changing makes you wishy-washy. In reality, though, many people *want* to be doing the same, changing their own paths in life, but they don't for fear of being shamed. People stay in unhappy marriages, unfulfilling jobs, and with self-limiting beliefs for fear of what's on the other side.

Humans don't do well with gray areas, so it's understandable that some people won't understand how you can be into meditation and still identify as Christian—and that's okay, as long as *you* get it. It's the consequence of being radically honest and being human. The only difference is Unruly ladies acknowledge it. The key is you have to be aware that you can be perceived like this. You have to be aware of how this lifestyle could come off to other people. And notice I said *be aware*; you don't necessarily have to care. And honestly, you shouldn't! Shout-out to Brené Brown, who taught us that we do care what people think, but we only have to care what *certain* people think. I love her metaphor of only considering the opinions of other people that are in the arena with you. Let the cheap seats talk, but don't let their opinions and voices get inside your head. Don't let them dictate how you live your life. My dad used to say opinions are like assholes; everybody has one. There will never be a shortage of opinions about your life. If you let outside opinions become your guidance, then you will be disconnected from your sense of self and end up feeling utterly lost and aimless because people's opinions are fickle and change often. Instead, focus on who you know yourself to be and what you know you want.

Any person who's healthy and evolving changes their mind over time. You absolutely have your core values that will stay pretty much the same throughout your life, but other parts of you will evolve as you learn life lessons and as your needs in life change. Being able to disagree with yourself indicates a level of intellectual growth, adaptability, and integrity. You are not becoming a different person; you are growing more into who you are. You are agreeing to engage with yourself and the world in a critical, honest way.

For example, I was born in April, and I'm an Aries. Typically, people know the Aries for being represented by the ram, but Aries is also represented by the lamb. Spiritual teacher and author Audrye Arbe reminded me of the quiet power embodied in the metaphorical lamb. How this shows up in my life is that I can be highly passionate and fiery about something but also really emotional and sensitive about the same thing. My friends call me a *sensitive thug* because how are you the loudest person in the room but also the most sensitive? Understandably, this duality can confuse people, but being understood is not your primary goal. Your goal is to honor all aspects of yourself. The fact that I know this about myself now means I can curate when I perform the lamb and when I perform the ram. In my preparations for The Unruly Retreat I am a ram, uncompromising and driven. When I am at the retreat, I am the lamb, submitting to the will of the collective experience. Certain people don't ever get to see the lamb side of me because they do not know what to do with it or how to treat it properly. Certain people will never see the ram because it could be harmful to them and to our relationship with each other. This is the essence of Main Character Energy. I'm aware of how I may be perceived, but I don't always have to care, because I'm being true to myself—and I'm accepting of my "mess" in a healthy way, accepting of all of the different parts of me that make me . . . me. I'm the main character of my story, without centering other people's feelings about it over my own.

Unruly Unquiry

- What situations or life circumstances (mess) are you holding on to that inspire shame or guilt? What mistakes keep you up at night, wishing you could have done something differently?

- What would your life look like if you lovingly accepted your mess as a meaningful part of your life's journey? What version of yourself could finally live?

DEVELOP YOUR MAIN CHARACTER ENERGY

Now that you're aware of what Main Character Energy is and why it's needed to embark on this Unruly journey, it's time to develop it. I acknowledge that not everyone has immeasurable confidence in themselves. You may feel intimidated by the idea of being the main character in your life and prioritizing your wants, needs, and desires. But to unearth your authentic self and live a life that truly brings you happiness, you have to care more about *you* than you do anyone else. Again, this doesn't make you selfish or egotistical; it makes you a better person to the important people in your life. It's worth it to dig deep into who you are and openly express all the things that make you, you.

Step One: Say Their Names

Every version of yourself that you have ever been lives inside of you, and they all want your attention—this is where it can get messy. It can be confusing to walk through life with different versions of yourself, with different wants and needs vying for your attention. All while you're just trying to get through your day. To keep track of it all, it helps to give these different versions of ourselves a name and distinguishable personality traits.

If your life is a performance, you are the actor, but you play many different roles over the course of a life. You've performed as many different characters (aspects of self) over time. Each aspect of our self has her own origin story, purpose, and characteristics. If you are not firmly directing the show, sometimes these different characters (all of whom are part of you) go to war with each other, perhaps even acting in ways that go against your highest self-interest. This is generally where the discomfort and irritation of living an inauthentic life comes from, as these aspects of self compete for control and attention instead of working harmoniously together. Giving them a name will bring them out of the shadows and into the light so you may direct the show appropriately.

During one particular session with my therapist, I expressed some internal frustration and that I didn't know where it was coming from. She asked me, "What version of Shelah am I speaking to right now?" Then she asked me to stop for a moment and identify every version of myself that ever existed. *What?* I thought. *What does that even mean?* She broke it down like this: From the time we are born until now, we grow through many versions of ourselves. They may be around for only a couple weeks or months, but they are clear indicators of the many women and girls we've ever been and the roles we've played throughout life.

Every time you've had a major transition that required you to change, that meant you had to develop a new version of yourself and be reborn. Think about it: Were you the same person at age five as you were at age twelve? Did you like the same things? Engage with the same people? Play the same roles in your family? When I reflected back through my entire life, I realized there were many times where I felt I had to change. Over the course of several sessions, I created a list of all the characters I've ever played from in utero until the present day. My list looked something like this:

- Womb Shelah: hanging out in my mom's womb

- Newborn Shelah: parents still together, but it's chaotic

- Post-Divorce Shelah: adjusting to living in a house without my dad

- Child Shelah: adjusting to a new stepdad

- Big Sister Shelah: my sister, Tiffany, was born at the same time my older sister moved away

And so on. By the end of my brainstorm session, I had come up with twelve different versions of me, or archetypes.

In the theater, archetypes help us understand a character's purpose in the narrative, and in this process, they can do the same for you. Ignoring or repressing your archetypes would mean you never really take center stage in your own life. You don't ever give yourself the opportunity to know yourself intimately enough to perform authentically. Instead, you re-perform what you've done in the past or what you think will please others. And on the flip side, letting certain archetypes overrule others can lead to an energetic imbalance in the way you carry yourself and even interact with others. In order to learn them, you must acknowledge them.

"But why name them?" you may ask.

When I was in the middle of writing this book, I went to a gala-style dinner, and introduced myself to a woman at my table. I saw she was wearing a nameplate necklace in a language I wasn't familiar with, so I struck up a conversation.

"What does that say?" I asked.

"It says Wednesday. That's my name." She went on to explain that in the place where she was from in Ghana, people are named after the day of the week they are born. She said you can tell many things about her by her name: what day of the week she was born, where her parents are from, and the circumstances of her birth. Her name introduces her to the world. Her name gives context for her existence.

Similarly, naming your character helps you to understand her purpose and performance. In this exercise, you are going to name all the archetypes that have ever lived within you. In the words of Iyanla Vanzant, "Call a thing a thing, Beloved!"

As you begin to acknowledge and name the different versions of yourself, your mess, proceed in a way that feels good to you, but also challenges you. By doing so, you will actually become really good friends with yourself through intimately getting to know yourself. These qualities live inside you and impact your life, whether you acknowledge them or not. It's much more empowering to intentionally call these versions of yourself to come to the stage in a harmonious way, as opposed to them performing what they choose to at will, without your understanding.

In your journal, make a list of the different versions of you. You created a new version of yourself each time you felt you had to become a new person. For example: I was Womb Shelah, hanging out in my mom's womb, until the next major shift, being born. At that point Newborn Shelah was created. The next big shift for me was my parents' divorce. Then my mom remarrying, and so on. This may take some time, but that's okay; you are getting to know yourself and that doesn't need to be rushed. Honor yourself for taking the time to get reacquainted with yourself in such an intentional way. Feel free to get creative and personal with the names. They should be easy to understand and provide context for the character. For example: If your archetype was chronically misunderstood, maybe she's Miss Misunderstood. If she felt left out all the time, maybe a good name for her is The Odd One Out. Or if she was scolded for being too loud, she could be The Loud One.

The Weird One
Here's an example of how I came to name one of my archetypes. You may have already guessed by now from my tidying-up story, but I am a neat freak. Period. I *love* cleaning. It calms me. When life feels out of control, there's always a rage cleaning session to calm me down. Funnily enough, though, I also have a bathroom phobia—well, a public bathroom phobia. I really just don't like germs, and if I could, I would never go in a public bathroom if I didn't have to, ever. Why am I telling you this? Because *takes a deep breath in because I can't believe I'm saying this out loud* I spent most of my eighth-grade year in the gross-ass middle school bathroom. Doing what, you ask?
Eating lunch.

Yes, you read that right. I was eating Lunchables in a public bathroom thanks to intense social anxiety. By the time I got to middle school, it was very clear to me that fitting in was not going to be something that was easy for me. Middle school is already the apex of social anxiety. Everyone is clumsily wading through angst and trying to find their place in a group of peers. It can be a challenging time for any middle schooler, and I was no exception to that rule.

I didn't start out eating lunch in the bathroom, but by this age I had already learned to hide. I had learned to hide parts of myself and my home life in order to avoid awkward moments with my peers. Eighth grade was when I started to really notice how much race would affect my experience in the world. I always knew that I was different, but it was really starting to become apparent because I was feeling pressure to make impossible choices from my peers: Are you Cuban? Are you Black? Which group would I join?

I really couldn't reconcile with the choosing because it meant that I had to deny parts of myself that were very real and alive. How could I choose between my mom's heritage and my dad's? I knew I was a mix of both, and I wasn't necessarily in favor of denying one for the other. Instead, I just started avoiding everybody.

I remember one time after step team practice my mom came to pick me up. I had already given my mom explicit pick-up instructions: please pick me up all the way at the end of the parking lot, away from all of my friends so that nobody would see me getting picked up by my mom. I was trying to avoid having any conversations about why my mom looked like she was, in the words of one of my friends, "My nanny." My mom was mistaken a lot for being some version of Latina, or "spicy white" as they say now. I just wanted my family to all look like me, like most of my friends. So, I gave my mom those very clear pick-up instructions and asked her, "Whatever you do—at all costs—do not drive up to the front of the school."

Well, you know my rebellious spirit that I love so much? Yeah, I got it from my mama. One thing about her: she does not follow rules. And she absolutely wasn't going to follow rules from me. And so my mom, being very on brand, pulled up to the front of the parking lot and started screaming my name out of the car window.

"Shelaahhhhh! Shelahhhhhhh! Get your ass in the car!"

My worst fears were being realized. Mind you, I was just getting out of step practice with all of my friends (who were all Black), whose opinions felt like life or death to my kid brain. We were closing out practice, and I faintly heard my mom's voice yelling my name from across the school campus. To make matters worse, I didn't get to the car fast enough, so she came looking for me. ON CAMPUS! I saw her walking up, and I panicked.

"Mom, what are you doing? I told you not to come up here! Go back in the car!" I yelled.

If you are fortunate enough to have ever seen a BET movie, there's always this moment where a character is in a crazy situation and the entire scene freezes. Then you hear the voiceover of the main character saying, "Yeah, that's me. You're probably wondering how I got here." I'm pretty sure that's what went through my friends' heads because they looked absolutely stunned—no, terrified. My friends snapped their heads on their necks like they saw a ghost and literally gasped out loud. They were certain I was about to get the whooping of a lifetime right in front of the entire step team for talking back to my mom with so much attitude.

"That's your . . . mom?" my friend Karla asked with her head titled to one side.

In my mind, I thought that they were responding to my mom not looking like me, but they were really responding to the way I'd raised my voice at my mother. And in that second, I internalized a hefty amount of shame about myself. I was ashamed that I did talk to my mother like that. I was ashamed that that was an impulse, and I was more ashamed that I didn't know better. This was another signifier that I was not raised in a Black household.

It's common knowledge in Black communities that in Black households you *never* raise your voice at your mother, and *especially* not in front of company. But in my household, we all screamed. It was a screaming match every single day, all day. We were loud. My mom screamed at us, my stepdad screamed back, and the dog cussed us all out. It was a sport, and I excelled at it, even more as I approached my teens. I wasn't proud of my behavior. Truthfully, I was ashamed. I didn't like acting that way, but I also didn't have the tools to change my behavior. I did not have any models for healthy communication or managing my emotions. This even translated to adulthood, where I had trouble recognizing that some people consider raising your voice or yelling to be a symptom of a problem or that there's a conflict or an issue. But for me, that's just how people communicated.

The car ride home was silent. I sat with a heavy weight of shame on my shoulders the entire way, and I wanted to literally leave my body. I wanted to just be able to perform correctly. I wanted to be able to have my mom pick me up from the front of the school with no problem. I wanted to be able to eat my lunch in the cafeteria with everybody else. But that wasn't my journey. I already didn't invite friends over to my house for this specific reason—that and the fact that my stepfather was a victim of a severe alcohol addiction. He would get blackout drunk like clockwork every Friday, which would create a domino effect of events that would end in the police being called. The police came to our house so much that they knew all of our names. I knew that I wanted to hide that from my friends as much as possible.

At school, at least, I could pretend that I was somewhat normal. Over-performing in school became my way of overcompensating for the chaos that I lived through every day. I was living a lie, because I didn't know what to do with all the shame I had about my mess. My home life was a disaster, but it was cool because I was a straight-A student. I was a shit-show at home, but in school I was vice president of Student Council. At home we sometimes had to eat from food pantries, but at school I was in the elite Gifted and Talented Program. At home, my house was always in a state of disarray, but at school I was on one of the best step teams in our county. I was kinda normal at school. Or so I thought. Because kids are more intelligent than we think, and they can smell a fraud from a mile away. And no matter how hard I tried, I really didn't fit into any group good enough to pass. My mess was in the way.

It was around this time when my mom took me to see a therapist because I was—*checks notes*—"hanging around too many Black kids." The session aimed to figure out why I just couldn't hang with my perfectly fine white friends. My mom wanted to know why I was suddenly interested in all of these Black things.

"Being on the step team has to be bad for her feet and joints," she told the therapist. "She's using slang now. The other day, she wrote 'cuz' instead of 'because.' I'm just worried about where all of this is going."

It was also around this time that I started giving myself box perms in my bathroom, successfully ruining my hair every six weeks like clockwork. I didn't have anyone around me who had hair like me or who could teach me how to do my hair, and I just wanted to be like my other friends. But of course, this backfired epically, and I have the yearbook picture to prove it. My edges did not join me in said yearbook photo. The consequence of all of this was I started to develop what I now know as anxiety. But at the time, I just thought I worried a lot. I would get stomachaches all the time, and no one could figure out what was wrong with me. I started to become terrified of the social aspect of school. The only time I felt really accepted and at peace was inside the classroom.

My mom gave me the best gift she could've ever given me when she signed me up for a highly selective school that was outside of my school district. The school was such in high demand that people in our neighborhood would put their kids on the waiting list when they were born in the hopes that they would get a spot by the time they were ready for kindergarten. I got into the school because I tested into the Gifted and Talented program. There were very few other non-Black children in most of my classes, three at the most. As an adult, I look back and see that these environments are potentially elitist, and I think there is a critique there for sure, but as a child, I just felt *special*. My teachers were excellent. They told me that I could be anything I wanted to be. They paid particular attention to my strengths and my weaknesses. My English teacher knew that I loved to read, so she would assign me extra books to read—which many kids would feel was a punishment but for me it felt like a privilege. I would arrive at school early and stay late to help teachers. I remember one time I arrived at school so early that the janitor hadn't even arrived to open the door.

School was where I found peace. School was where someone told me that I was worthy. School was where adults poured into me, where adults nurtured me. Raising my hand to answer questions gave me that serotonin boost that I needed to get through the day. Turning in an assignment and getting 100 percent reminded me that I was worthy of being heard.

I started to really wrap my identity around this idea of me being a star student. It was one thing I knew I could be good at instead of being "bad," "a brat," "spoiled," and all around—as my young brain saw it—a burden. This really hurt me at the time because I wanted to be helpful; I had already curated my identity around being useful and helpful because I wasn't sure if I could be "good," but I knew I could be useful. Whether it was cooking and cleaning at home or always being a helpful resource to my friends, I would go out of my way to be serviceable. But no matter how much I tried to be helpful at home, it didn't seem to ever help much. If anything, it made things worse, bringing me negative attention rather than positive.

As a response, I developed this burning anger—no, rage. Anger is a secondary emotion. Usually, underneath the anger is hurt or fear. For me, anger was a more acceptable emotion on its surface. It read as less weak than hurt or fear, which might make you less of a target. This anger within me grew like a shield or a mask. Whenever I felt that hurt or vulnerability coming in, the rage would swoop in to protect me. This made me a very angry young lady. Especially in middle school. The further I got from the school campus and the closer I got to my house, the more I knew I was leaving the good version of myself that I really liked and entering the shadow side of myself. The Angry Shelah.

So, when I was at school, I ate lunch in the bathroom to savor this peace and avoid conflict with my peers. Every now and then someone would walk in, see me eating food in the bathroom, and give a very normal reaction: "What are you doing? That's disgusting. Your whole lunch is gonna taste like pee." And they were right—it was disgusting, but it was also safe for me. That's how desperate I was to escape rejection.

Unfortunately, I never had the opportunity to address the root of my fear of rejection, so it followed me into adulthood in a variety of ways. For example, when I submitted my manuscript to my publisher for the first time, I knew it wasn't my best work, but I had to meet my deadline. Without knowing it, I was metaphorically still eating in the bathroom. I had deleted so much of my writing (hiding myself) because I felt it wasn't good enough (fear of rejection). If I really put myself into the manuscript, then I would also be vulnerable to be judged. I knew that I was in for feedback; that's an expected part of the process. And honestly, the feedback that I got was mild in comparison to what my mind had conjured up. My editor had given me thoughtful, comprehensive, appropriate feedback. Nothing in there that should've alarmed me, nothing extreme.

But it wasn't present-day Shelah reading that feedback. I was in the eighth grade, and I was getting rejected. And in her mind, any feedback less than amazing meant she wasn't smart. If I'm not smart, what am I? If my editor is telling me that I am not smart, then what is my actual purpose here? Feedback had brushed up against my open wound of not being good enough, and not being accepted. Also propping up this experience is the knowing that after this book leaves my hands, I can't control how it will be received. It is the ultimate in opening yourself up for rejection.

Through many nights of self-reflection, I was able to identify that the feeling of being misunderstood and experiencing rejection had a strong correlation with the middle-school version of myself. I call her The Weird One because she always stood out no matter how hard she tried to fit in. She always knew she was different from other children, and she quickly learned that not fitting in could make her more susceptible to rejection. So, in preempting that rejection, she often rejected others first. Before anyone could get the chance to call her weird, she created a circumstance to push people away. For The Weird One, it was better to orchestrate rejection on her terms rather than to let someone else do it. I could trace evidence of this type of rejection throughout my life, as rejection is a part of the human experience. However, my schema of being misunderstood/rejected has its most robust roots during elementary school. When I think of the genesis of The Weird One, I remember choosing to eat lunch in the girls' bathroom to avoid socializing with my classmates. While that image makes adult Shelah cringe substantially, I can understand that The Weird One was doing her best to avoid situations of public rejection (the lunchroom).

Take a moment to still the mind with the following meditation and identify the names of your archetypes based on the list you created. Focus on one at a time.

Meditation Moment

Find a quiet space where you can relax your mind and body. Take a few deep breaths to regulate your nervous system and close your eyes. One by one, imagine the versions of yourself you identified in step one. Take a moment to picture her in physical form. She can appear human, nonhuman, or as an animal—whatever feels right to you.

Look into her eyes and feel her warm and familiar gaze. Ask her, "What is your name?" Listen for a name that will help you identify what she *represents*—not a name like Wendy or Ruth but a name that will point to her function as one of your archetypes, like Reject, Eccentric, or People-Pleaser. Trust that the answer you receive is the right one.

If you couldn't hear their names during the meditation, that's okay; you can choose one by answering the following questions: What function did this version of you have? How did they try to keep you safe? What feeling were they trying to help you avoid? Remember, this is *your mess*, so you can always change the name later if you need to. You get to choose.

....

Step Two: Tell Her Story

Refer back to your list of characters. Start from the beginning and add a sentence or two to each character, telling her story. Her story should include when she was created; in my case, The Weird One was created during sixth-grade lunch period. Her story should also include why she was created; in my case, The Weird One was created to protect me from rejection. It doesn't matter if she was successful at her job or not—you just want to note the intention behind why you created her. She was created explicitly for this purpose.

My story would be: The Weird One was born in the bathroom during sixth-grade lunch period. She was created to *protect me from rejection*.

Take a moment to write the story of all the characters that live within you.

Step Three: Feel Her

This may be the most crucial step in this process. These characters bring emotional states with them, and for a reason. The way you feel when this character shows up will point to what you need in the present moment. If you can identify what she makes you feel, you can then take the appropriate care of both of you. During his research on facial expressions and emotions during the 1970s, American psychologist Paul Ekman identified that we generally have the following basic emotions: surprise, sadness, fear, disgust, anger, and joy.[1] These basic emotions lay the foundation for more complex emotional states that we experience, like amazement, loneliness, insecurity, shame, disappointment, humiliation, and pride, among many others. In the case of The Weird One, she felt a cocktail of emotions like sadness, shame, and fear of rejection. It's important to tap into the feelings of your avatar so you can identify where these emotions are still present within you today.

Now it's your turn. What is the primary emotion this character brings with her? Lead with curious researcher energy (think to yourself, *Hmm, this is interesting. What's going on here?*) and not judge-and-jury energy. ("I must get to the bottom of this and make a judgment.")

Your statement should look something like this:

What happened: I ate lunch in the bathroom. The Feeling: I felt shameful, lonely, and afraid.

Step Four: Nurture Her

Your mess is a part of your intelligent design and was created for a reason, often representing an unmet need in your past. In my case, The Weird One was designed to protect me. I knew I was empathetic and prone to getting hurt feelings, so in my mind, rejecting someone first was less painful than being rejected myself. Her function was to remind me of this unmet need, and knowing this now gives me the opportunity to finally fulfill it.

What unmet need are the versions of you from step two asking you to nurture? In what way is your current discomfort a signal that you need to nurture yourself in this moment?

Everything has a function; we reduce, reuse, and recycle parts of ourselves. We are not wasteful by design. So, why are each of these archetypes showing up for you in your life? The answer is: You need something, and they are there to try to help you fulfill it.

Use the following sentence as your guide:
When I feel _____ [feeling from step three], I am reminded that I need _____ [nurture the need].

Now that you're aware of what your characters want and need, take a moment to ask yourself how to best nurture those needs. Do something that makes you feel loved, safe, confident, heard, seen, appreciated, etc. If you're having trouble coming up with an answer, use the following list as inspiration.

- Be curious. Ask her what she needs as opposed to demanding that she leave.

- Engage your creative side. Move, draw, paint, sing.

- Affirm her. Praise her the way you would a child.

- Connect with nature. Put your bare feet on the earth, put your hands in the dirt, touch a tree.

- Remember your body. Engage your five senses with a bath, massage, meal, or music. Get out of your head and into your body.

- Meditate.

- Masturbate.

- Take a nap.

Step Five: Your Ensemble

Bravo! You have just created your Main Character Ensemble. You now have a deeper understanding of the different versions of yourself and are on your way to performing them in harmony. Now when you reach an emotionally uncomfortable moment, you have a plan for how to care for yourself. For example, a part of why I created the Unruly experience is because of The Weird One, because I chose to dance with her instead of hiding her. She doesn't fit in because she wasn't meant to, and those circumstances created Curly, Curvy, Conscious and The Unruly Retreat.

Exploring your archetypes, or characters, and honoring your inner diversity by acknowledging your shadow selves, is a form of self-integration, an act of recovering repressed aspects of who you are to achieve a deeper level of inner wholeness. Your power lies in highlighting the uniqueness of each archetype, or character, in harmony with their counterparts. The goal is for you to perform as your own ensemble through these archetypes. You are your own one-woman show, the Main Character in your story. The goal is for you to intentionally choose when to embody each archetype instead of allowing them to exit and enter the stage unexpectedly.

The next time you experience unwanted or difficult emotions, challenge yourself to take a step back and name which member of your ensemble is performing. Resist the urge to judge yourself and the experience and, instead, focus on her needs and greater purpose. Treat each moment as an opportunity to explore what need is not being met within. There is always a lesson to learn.

Take tiny moments in your day to take inventory of when your archetypes show up, almost like a game. After a while, they start to feel like old friends instead of intrusive guests. "Oh, there's The Weird One. Hey girl!"

Meditation Moment

If you ever find yourself out of harmony with one of your archetypes, take a moment to complete the following mini meditation.

Sit or lay down in a comfortable position and close your eyes. Imagine you are standing in front of a door. On the other side of the door, you will meet the archetype you are out of harmony with. On the count of three, open the door and enter the home of that archetype.

See her calmly and quietly engaged in an activity. What is she doing? Take a moment to observe her in silence. Now, ask her, "What do you need right now?" Give yourself permission to hear a clear, simple answer, then visualize her getting exactly what she needs, even if you don't know how it will happen. As you do this, imagine that you are *also* getting exactly what you need. Take a few minutes to sit in this. How does it feel to have your needs met? What thoughts or sensations are flowing through your mind and body? Your archetype smiles at you, you both wave goodbye, and you find yourself at the same door you entered at the beginning of this mediation. On the count of three, you will be on the other side of the door.

Learning to dance with all aspects of who you are allows you to move through the world with more authenticity, dynamism, and integrity. Although this process doesn't happen overnight and it certainly isn't a walk in the park, on the other side lies deep personal power that you can call on to connect more deeply with yourself. In the next chapter, we'll dive into self-compassion, which is a concept that will help you fully step into the main character you are.

Repeat after me: I choose to live in harmony with all aspects of myself.

Unperform

5

Compassionate Character Study

Now that you have absorbed how your Main Character Energy plays a role in your life, it's time for the next step toward Unruly-ness: compassion. You have a better familiarity with your present-day self, as well as the cast of characters that perform within you. Now I ask you, is what you/they are performing true? We are all performing all the time on this stage called life, but what is the content of the show? Instead of performing, which prioritizes the opinion of an audience, I challenge you to move toward *unperforming*. Unperforming is undoing, untangling, and unmasking yourself from everything that stands in the way of you and truth. In order to do that, you must exercise compassion. I unexpectedly began learning this lesson several years ago while sitting on the A train, in Brooklyn of all places.

"When someone commits a crime at home, our first thought is how we might have failed that person," my Gambian roommate, Nyjambou, said as we headed into the city to 14th Street on the A train. While I lived in Brooklyn, in a shared brownstone apartment that we affectionately called The Long Hallway, I was lucky to share space with artists, directors, and scholars from India, France, Palestine, South Africa, and beyond, as we saw many roommates come and go. The vibe of our home was a little hippie, a little commune-ish, with a dash of girl-boss energy and a heavy creative slant. When Nyjambou moved in one summer, she and I grew particularly close. We would often take West African dance classes together in Manhattan, and on the way home from dance one day, we got on the topic of prison reform. Nyjambou told me she didn't understand Americans' thought process when it came to punishment and rehabilitation. From her Swedish perspective (where she was raised), people in jails made a wrong choice, but they were not necessarily bad people. To her, the American consciousness, on the other hand, generally frames people who commit crimes as criminals. Forever. But the harsh reality is, in jails across America, there are "criminals" who are also victims of trauma, people who could not access mental health care when they needed it, and people who, with the appropriate rehabilitative care, could be a great benefit to our society. This is a very simplistic approach to the differences between Swedish and American culture, as there are many other components to consider. Still, the core concept of redemption after harm is worth exploring.

The critical difference between these two ways of thinking is simple. One has compassion for another person's experience, and the other does not. I would argue that many of us replicate this draconian style of justice in our own minds: When we make a mistake, we give ourselves the harshest punishment possible, making ourselves pay for one transgression countless times. We hold the error so close to us that, sometimes, it becomes a part of our identity. This mindset breeds a cycle of guilt and shame and stunts your overall growth.

We might not be able to reform the American prison system so it operates from a place of humanity or compassion, although I would love to see that in my lifetime, but we can always begin the process of reforming our own sense of justice. Unruly women need to give themselves an extra dose of self-compassion because we are more likely to make what we perceive as "mistakes" in the eyes of society. We are more likely to step outside normative expectations, challenge unhealthy dynamics, and pose difficult questions. Because of this, we are bound to encounter conflicts and misunderstandings with others—and within ourselves. So you must go easy on yourself so that you can keep unperforming and clearing what doesn't serve you.

> **Self-compassion: a gentle and sympathetic and honest engagement with your thoughts, beliefs, feelings, and actions.**

Compassion sounds like this cutesy, warm-and-fuzzy experience—but it's actually serious work. Compassion allows us to do hard things. To look at hard things. To examine hard things. And to do one of the hardest things ever—forgive ourselves. As we've learned, compassion is not only about forgiving ourselves when we do something we think we shouldn't; it's also being able to access kindness, understanding, *and* honesty simultaneously. One of the best ways to track your relationship with self-compassion is to pay attention to your inner monologue. When you make a perceived mistake, what does your inner voice say to you? Does she degrade you and talk to you harshly? Or does she speak to you gently and with understanding? If you find yourself being very inflexible and judgmental when you don't get things exactly right, chances are you're in a compassion drought.

Most of us treat ourselves harshly, doling out the maximum punishment for a perceived crime, whereas with self-compassion, we can be more like Nyjambou and acknowledge both the transgression *and* the circumstances that created it. This approach leaves more room for growth, making it easier for you to stay on your journey long term.

I had a crash course in self-compassion the year I agreed to do *Love & Hip Hop Miami* (2022). My husband and I had declined several offers for reality television in the past, having a full understanding of how the genre has perpetuated negative stereotypes about Black people. But finally, after a ton of meetings, meditations, and spiritual guidance, we said yes to filming one season of the reality show. I knew, to an extent, what I was getting myself into—or at least I thought I knew. I knew of the show's problematic history. I knew all the reasons why I should say no. But what *really* confused me was the fact that, internally, I was being guided to say yes. My own inner guidance, and the guidance of the people around me whom I really respect, was somehow leading me toward a yes. This period was so confusing for me because I did not understand at all why I was feeling like this was something that I should do, when logically and intellectually I was thinking, *Shelah, this is an absolute no.*

But I decided to follow my intuition, even though I was still hesitant. As soon as filming started, I quickly realized this would be harder to navigate than I'd assumed. *But I'm evolved*, I thought. *I'm smart*, I told myself. *I can control how this goes.*

Spoiler alert: I *could not* control how things went. I was exhausted from the mental labor of constantly trying to figure out what someone was *really* saying or what their *real* intentions were because I knew I couldn't trust anything at face value—which is not the experience I am used to. I have made the specific choice to spend little time around people whose intentions I can't trust. In my everyday life, if I feel like I can't trust you, you will not have guaranteed access to me. I will politely exit stage left. I have absolutely no energy to do guesswork; if I feel a weird vibe from someone, I will simply create distance and let them figure it out. If someone is in my inner circle and we have a strong foundation, then there will be more conversations, but generally speaking, I ain't got time. It was no secret that previous guests on the show had spoken out about their less-than-positive experiences with producers, so I knew sneaky behavior was a possibility.

Unbeknownst to me, I had started filming while I was pregnant. So there was this whole roller coaster that I was going on right at the time that I started filming. My husband and I went from ecstatic about our first pregnancy to talking about how we were going to hide it from producers. Understandably, we wanted to keep it to ourselves for as long as possible, at least for the first twelve weeks so we could ensure the pregnancy would be viable.

But those producers were cunning and vigilant; this wasn't their first rodeo. They knew immediately what was up when I cancelled a scene for a "medical emergency." I will give them credit—they were very kind to me when I finally told them, and they did move forward with grace and a level of compassion regarding the miscarriage topic. But it was still reality TV, and in this context, my trauma was other people's entertainment. It's still a business after all. I didn't even have a moment to process the grief of the miscarriage before I had to start filming again. I think I was back in filming two days after my miscarriage. I wasn't ready. Honestly, if I had known I was pregnant, I wouldn't have signed on to film initially because I knew I would need that space for myself. But I was already in it.

When I look back, I laugh at how I was so critical and yet so naive at the same time. I thought I would be doing something I could be proud of—sharing my grief in real time, offering space for women on a similar journey. My inner voice now says, *I mean, yes girl, you could have in the right context, but you forgot where you were. These viewers don't want a deep dive into your emotional life. They want a snippet and then soundbites and an easy-to-follow, lightly petty storyline.* I had the right idea, but in the wrong context. Right performance, wrong stage.

When the show aired, I was mortified. I felt like I was watching myself in a funhouse mirror. Except it wasn't fun. It's one thing to show somebody struggling through things, and then balancing it out with moments of them being fun, witty, or cute. That diverse image gives someone humanity. But what I saw of myself as I was portrayed on that show was flat, one-sided, and distorted. There was no evidence of my humor, lightheartedness, goodwill, or the deep way in which I support my husband. And there was absolutely nothing I could do about it. What's done is done.

So there I was watching the worst parts of myself on TV every week and in my day-to-day life trying to figure out why I had miscarried and what our next steps were as a couple. I had been thinking that in order to be spiritually aligned, all I had to do was focus on the good, peaceful, and happy things in life. But exposing the self-identified worst parts of my personality gave me a choice. I could lament about it, or I could choose to use the moment to do some major shadow work. Having anxiety was my main talking point on the show, which was reflected in the editing. I seemed to say the word "anxiety" in almost every single green-screen interview that aired. My very real mental health struggles were now watered down to fit a storyline.

When I looked on the screen and saw myself, it did not feel like a full human was being reflected back at me.

So I decided that the only way I was going to make this experience worthwhile was to use it to heal anything about my life on the screen that I didn't like. I did not like being defined by my anxiety. I used all of that embarrassment, shame, and guilt to begin healing myself more deeply. I used it as an opportunity to investigate how I could go beyond my current relationship with anxiety. I restarted therapy and put a special focus on compassion for myself.

My experience on the show is directly responsible for me healing my relationship with anxiety. This was a MAJOR achievement for me. I now experience anxiety like a visitor, like the way I do my family. *Knock, knock. Oh, hey girl. That's right, I was expecting you—I know you come to visit sometimes. You can stay for a little while, but you cannot live here.* My family already knows they cannot pop in unannounced. No shade, but you cannot come over here to my house without advance notice. And also, when you come to my house, you have to let me know how long you're staying. I'm very protective of my environment. So if I'm protective over my home environment like that, why wouldn't I be protective over my mental environment?

On the other side of all that shame and guilt was freedom. The freedom to tell a truer story. I am not a walking posterboard for anxiety. I am not any of the labels that society places on me. On the other side of that most public performance was the opportunity to unperform, to shed any old baggage that I no longer needed. Life is so much more liberating—and easy—when it's true.

Unruly Inquiry

Think back to a time when you needed to show yourself compassion but didn't. How did you feel in that moment? Was the harshness helpful, or did it hinder you in the long run?

WHAT ABOUT IT? A QUICK COMPASSIONATE LIFE HACK

Before moving to Florida, my mom spent the formative years of her childhood in New Jersey, so she adopted a New Jersey accent with a Boston twang, thanks to my grandmother. My mother has always had a sharp, snappy, and funny way about her, and looking back, the thing I grew to admire most about her was the moments when she was utterly unapologetic during a perceived misstep. One time we were in the checkout line at the grocery store, and she was painstakingly gathering coupons for the cashier. It seemed like it was taking an eternity. I could hear the exaggerated deep breaths of the cashier, who couldn't outright say, "Hurry up, lady!" But being the hypersensitive child who had learned to attune myself to others, I picked up on the nonverbal communication from the cashier and the line behind us. Feet shuffling, heavy sighing, and bodies shifting to better gauge my mom's progress all clued me in that their patience was running thin. As a result, I got increasingly anxious, and the people-pleaser in me started to genuinely worry about inconveniencing the people behind us.

"Are you gonna take all day?" one of the customers finally challenged from the end of the line.

In her perfect mob wife-esque New Jersey accent, without ever diverting her gaze from her coupon wallet, my mother said, "And what if I am? What about it?"

That was it. That was the end of it. And what was the worst that could happen? The other patrons had to wait an extra few minutes or go to a different line? Yes, my mom knew she was taking a long time in line, and ... what about it? My mom used those three simple words to diffuse what I thought would be a massive confrontation. She knew she was taking a long time, she acknowledged it, and now that ball was in their court. The person with the issue had to decide what they wanted to happen next.

To be clear, "What about it?" is not about placing a value judgment (making a thing "good" or "bad) on an encounter or naming anyone as right or wrong. It is simply a present-tense, nonjudgmental acknowledgment of your role in an exchange. "What about it?" says: Yes, I acknowledge my role in this present exchange. No, I am not placing a value judgment on myself right now. Now that we have that information, how would you like to move forward?

That last question can apply to yourself or someone else. Now, understand me clearly. I am not advocating for you to do whatever you want and then use the "What about it?" concept as a get-out-of-jail-free card. This is not a placeholder for self-accountability and integrity. What I am suggesting is that this is a valid and powerful form of self-compassion, and it is absolutely critical for building the skill of self-accountability and behavior modification moving forward. Many Unruly ladies have reported hyper-focusing on their mistakes, while not acknowledging their achievements with the same weight. This adherence to focusing on missteps creates a vicious cycle of stress and harshness.

Without even knowing it, by acknowledging and naming your mess and owning your faults, you've taken a playful approach to your own self-judgments, which allows you to now move past them. Now what? Use this moment to check in with yourself in your journal about the next best step you can take to move forward in a gentle and honest way.

Unruly Unquiry

Think of a time when you totally messed up, in your opinion. What happened?

- What did your inner voice say to you in that moment? How did others react?

- How did you feel hearing those things? Take a moment to think about how your inner monologue affects you.

- What would you have liked to hear from yourself at that moment?

Self-compassion acts as a lubricant to keep the gears of your personal development vehicle moving as smoothly as possible. I want you to remember that self-compassion is also a skill. The more you practice it, the better you'll get at it. The goal is not perfection; rather, the aim is to allow more space for expansion and gentleness in your life.

Now that you have a deeper capacity for understanding the importance of self-compassion, let's dive into how to put this idea into practice.

Repeat after me: I am gentle and honest with myself.

6

Self-Love in Action

"I think you should talk to them about that. I don't feel like they considered you at all at that moment. Girl, I would be pissed," I said during a FaceTime call with my close friend and the creative director of The Unruly Retreat, Tashah.

"But I'm not mad," she said after a pause. Oh shit, I'd offended her. I could tell by the change in the tone of her voice. This was not what I wanted.

"Well, I'm just saying—" I searched for something to say to make it better.

"Just because that's how you would feel doesn't mean I feel that way," she said in reply. "Anyway, let's talk about something else."

If you haven't noticed by now, I am a very opinionated young lady and always have been. I enjoy thoughtful discourse, I'm not afraid of disagreeing, and sharing my thoughts has always come naturally. But during that FaceTime call, it was clear that speaking out of turn and offering unsolicited advice had hurt my friend's feelings. On a subsequent call, she expressed to me that sometimes she wanted to just be able to share without getting advice in return. She wanted to talk to a friend, not be a guest on *Shelah Fix My Life*. I felt guilty for offending her. The people-pleaser in me was uncomfortable.

Here's where the importance of acceptance, not approval, comes in. I initially talked about this topic on the first "Meditation Mixtape" I recorded with a cheap podcast microphone on my laptop. I had no idea that recording myself in a closet would reach so many people. One of the most popular tracks is called "Acceptance," where I address the concepts laid out in this chapter.

The good news is you already have self-compassion as a foundation for the idea of acceptance. If self-love is the destination, acceptance is the vehicle. Not to be confused with approval, which is a misconception I see often, so let's draw a clear distinction between the two.

> **Approval implies making a value judgment about something. It is the act of labeling an action or an experience as desirable or not desirable.**

The problem with approval is that, by definition, it requires a dichotomy. One has to be right, and the other has to be wrong. It creates a victim and a perpetrator, and that dynamic, *which offers no healing*. A nonjudgmental approach is crucial for an Unruly lifestyle. In the case of the conversation with my friend, I could have left that conversation and immediately approved or disapproved of my actions, by saying something like: "I said nothing wrong; I was having a harmless dialogue" (approval), or "I was wrong for expressing unwanted opinions" (disapproval).

If I chose to approve of my actions, I would've subconsciously communicated to myself that I was the right one. As a result, there's no need to examine my behavior because I did nothing wrong, so the opportunity to grow from this moment is gone. If I chose to disapprove of my actions, then I would've subconsciously communicated to myself that I was wrong, which could easily lead to self-rejection. In this instance, I might judge myself for the exchange and then determine that I need to stop giving advice altogether because nobody wants to hear it.

Choosing between approval or disapproval is not a productive use of your time and will keep you from growing as needed. Determining who's right or wrong in a situation is also incredibly subjective and hardly ever finite. Many things can be true at the same time, and perspectives often change depending on the person's vantage point. But approval does not allow for nuance. Approval cuts off any possibility for new outcomes. A more productive approach for your Unruly journey is to practice acceptance.

ACCEPTANCE

If self-love is the noun, acceptance is the verb. Acceptance is self-love in action. Free from the confines of judgment, I could look more deeply at the encounter with my friend. I could listen to her without needing to defend myself or justify my actions. With gentle curiosity, I could explore what felt true for me. I could give myself permission to hear that she values me as a listening ear, but that doesn't mean she always wants my opinion on her life. And that's okay. It doesn't make anyone right or wrong.

> **Acceptance is embracing the present without needing to change it—*for now.***

Similarly, you can acknowledge the imperfections in yourself and your interactions with others without needing to change them. Yes, you are on a growth journey, but you are not here to be in a never-ending cycle of fixing, changing, and doing. If you're not careful, that mindset can divorce you from the experience of actually being yourself and seduce you into falling in love with a fictional, "perfect" future you. As Nathaniel Branden stated in his book *The Six Pillars of Self-Esteem*, "Self-acceptance is my refusal to be in an adversarial relationship to myself."[1]

Self-love is embodied in accepting ourselves exactly how we are and not how we think we should be. It shows us that we deserve love and grace at every stage of our self-love journey, not only when we get it "right." If we are always framing ourselves as needing fixing, we send the subconscious message that we are not okay as we are. It is one thing to have a growth mindset; it is another to force yourself to meet impossible standards. The goal is to accept everything you are right now and be open to improving.

Acceptance invites curiosity. Curiosity opens up possibilities for change.

There's a difference between "you should have known better" and "you know better than this—I wonder why you made that choice anyway." Acceptance leaves room to get curious about why you are where you are. Instead of a harsh, punishing energy, you use curiosity to move you closer to what you desire. There is deep strength in softness. You are no longer focusing on rejecting the present (I *should* have done XYZ) and instead focusing on why this is happening to you right now. You can't investigate your reality if you're judging it. It won't work because you will get discouraged and give up. Ironically, acceptance allows you to funnel all that energy you have toward a solution.

There's this myth that we need harshness to be motivated. That if you're too nice with yourself then you will get complacent where you are and not evolve. This could happen, but what is more likely is that the softness allows you to find deeper inspiration to move you forward in the long term. The softness inspires new possibilities. You find that you no longer fear disappointing yourself, so you take more chances. You're no longer hearing a rigid inner voice, so you hear yourself better. Acceptance is your secret weapon for doing hard things.

Meditation Moment

Sit or lie in a comfortable position and bring your awareness to the present moment. Focus on simply being here, right now. Don't try to mentally travel anywhere or feel any particular thing. Just allow yourself to be exactly as you are. When you are settled, repeat the phrase "I love you" out loud to yourself. If you're not in an environment to say it out loud, it's okay to say it in your head. Take a moment to see how your mind and body feel as you say these words. Now, place your hands over your heart and, again, repeat "I love you" to yourself for a few minutes. As you do this, notice any resistance you may feel. Know that however you are feeling is OK. Don't judge these sensations or try to justify them. Just keep repeating "I love you" to yourself until you feel complete.

When you've come out of your meditation, take a moment to consider the following questions in your journal:

Did you find any resistance within yourself as you said "I love you"? If so, where was this resistance in your body? How did it feel? Did it soften as you kept repeating the phrase, or did it linger long after the meditation was over?

Why do you think this resistance was present?

If you didn't experience resistance during this meditation, why do you think that is? How did it feel to say "I love you" to yourself?

....

As we came back from break on Day 3, I grabbed my coffee and headed down to the room where workshops were held. The ladies eagerly poured into session, some still in their yoga clothes, having just attended the morning yoga session. Some ladies sat cross-legged on a pillow or yoga mat, others sat in chairs with journals in tow.

I expressed to them that I was really happy that self-love is becoming a part of our common conversations and understanding of mental health. It's a great sign that we're openly talking about loving ourselves more without the stigma of selfishness tinging the air. But when a term gets absorbed into popular culture, it often loses its deeper meaning. Or rather, it can begin to take on many meanings at once.

I remember searching for the definition of self-love early on in my healing journey. I really wanted to know the metric for self-love. I knew I didn't have it, but how would I know when I did? How do I know if I'm actually loving myself? Acceptance is the only answer for me. In my experience, acceptance is the clearest metric for self-love. Accepting yourself exactly as you are in the current moment—your thoughts, beliefs, actions, and perceived mistakes—without needing to change yourself is an act of unconditional love.

"What would fully accepting yourself give you the permission to do? Who would you have the permission to be?" I asked the group.

"Limitless," said one woman.

"Free," said another.

"I definitely wouldn't tolerate no shit!" someone piped up. The group erupted in laughter.

Exactly!

THE 8 MILE EFFECT

One of my absolute favorite things about acceptance is that it gives you the *8 Mile* effect. You remember that scene from *8 Mile*? Where Eminem is in this rap battle and before the other guy can start his round, Eminem lays out all his own personal flaws. He automatically won the round because he accepted all of his own mess to the point that the other guy didn't have anything else to say. It was his story, and it was true. And that's what I want for you. The goal for this entire book is self-liberation. I want you to be able to be free from the harsh judgments that women face. Even the ones that have been internalized and feel like they are our own—these are ideas that have been socialized and programmed into us so thoroughly that we think that they came from us. We didn't just wake up one day and decide that a thin body frame with a small waist and a bigger bust and bigger hips is desirable. These things were socialized and programmed into us. Again, Crooked Room. When you accept all of your mistakes and your perceived flaws, you disarm other people from being able to weaponize them against you. The goal is to accept everything we are right now and be open to improving.

From this, we also start to realize how much of a judgmental voice we have with ourselves. I wanted to be able to share secrets with myself. I wanted to be able to tell myself my own deep, dark thoughts—to be able to openly express what I thought I *shouldn't* be doing or *shouldn't* be feeling. I wanted to be able to have a conversation with myself without being judged by myself. I had to lie to myself more to avoid my own judgment. I had to hide things from myself to avoid my own judgment. I thought I feared the world judging me, but the truth was, I was afraid of *my own* judgment. Make it make sense. We need to learn to quiet this judgmental voice within ourselves so we can have honest conversations with ourselves without having to be afraid of our own judgments.

Do you want to be right or do you want to be happy? Releasing myself from the need to be right is actually one of the most powerful tools I've ever harnessed and used. Can you find your place in the world without comparing yourself to someone else? There's a certain function that this black-and-white thinking has served for me in the past—shout out to Main Character Energy—but I'm older now; I'm more evolved, and I have more resources to draw upon to engage in complex thinking. The more I heal and move past my own triggers, the more I'm able to live in the gray area.

Meditation Moment

Take a few moments to center yourself with three deep breaths. When you're properly relaxed, say the following mantras to yourself out loud. If you can't say them out loud, you can state them in your mind instead.

I accept myself exactly as I am right now.

I am worthy of a happy, fulfilling life.

I am doing my best, and that is good enough.

I am always, at all times, exactly where I need to be.

As you speak these powerful, self-affirming mantras, take note of how you feel. Empowered? Joyful? Apprehensive? Uncomfortable? However you're feeling is completely valid. Don't try to revel in it too much, and don't try to push it away either. Just sit in the neutral state of observer. Continue to repeat these mantras to yourself for two to three minutes, making note of your body and mind's reactions. Regardless of how you feel, know that you deserve compassion and self-acceptance.

Acceptance Exercise: Acceptance Letter

Have you ever experienced or seen the excitement of a scholar receiving a letter of acceptance from an educational institution? I remember receiving my letter from Tisch and jumping on my bed like a child. I immediately called my parents and friends, announcing the good news: I had been formally accepted! While these moments of life are worthy of this level of excitement, why do we often reserve such joy for times where we are accepted by people outside ourselves? Well, I believe that learning to accept yourself exactly for who you are is worthy of a celebration too, despite a world that often convinces you otherwise.

So, in honor of yourself, I invite you to write a letter from yourself to yourself, informing you that you have been formally accepted. Feel free to use the following template as inspiration.

Dear _____,
[*Your Name*]

It is with great pleasure that I inform you that you have been formally accepted as being a woman worthy of her deepest desires. Congratulations on all the hard work you have done to reach this point. I feel that your [insert quality you love about yourself], your [another quality], and your [another quality] represent exactly the type of woman I desire to be. You no longer need to judge yourself harshly, overemphasize negative feedback, or reject the most special parts of who you are. You may now move through the world freer, lighter, and more authentically you. Once again, congratulations on this major achievement! I look forward to seeing what else you do in the world.

Sincerely, _____
[*Your Name*]

If you'd like, you can take this exercise a step further and plan a small celebration as many graduates do, like a dinner, a date, or a gathering with friends. You don't have to announce to them that you're having an acceptance celebration; that's totally up to you. You could frame it as an ordinary meetup, or let them in on your acceptance journey, whatever feels appropriate. Be sure to dress up nice and make yourself feel special, as this is absolutely a momentous occasion.

The distinction between acceptance and approval will allow you to see yourself and others more fully, as you won't immediately be searching for how you can fit an experience or person into a binary. Are they good or bad? Was I right or wrong? Instead, you'll realize the futility in approaching every dynamic with an either/or mentality. Sure, those binaries are useful and appropriate, as long as you have the ability to exist beyond them when you need to. But the more you practice this, the more you will see the nuances and complexities that make life interesting and engaging, and make people human. I felt it was necessary for you to have this foundation before getting into a more challenging aspect of healing: inner child work. Inner child healing will help you understand how scenarios that happened when you were a child still play out in your life today.

Repeat after me: I accept myself, exactly as I am, right now.

7

Passed-Down Performances

Now that we've spent some time exploring, understanding, and healing the *self* on our journey to deconstruct your Crooked Room, we need to take the time to consider how our family and community may have contributed to our present-day performance. Focusing solely on yourself when you're healing runs the risk of reinforcing a self-centered view about the world, which at its worst can make you critically isolated. The goal of healing is so you can exist safely in the world with others in a healthier way, not to reinforce an overly individualistic mindset. That type of mindset will always set you up for failure because we do not live in a vacuum.

Most of us desire familial connections, whether they be biological or chosen. There will be those who are lucky enough to not have had any childhood trauma, and in that case, you may graduate to the next chapter. But for those of you who had a less-than-desirable time as a child, this chapter is for you, as we will be exploring inner child healing. We may not have been able to choose our families or our early experiences, but we can choose how we respond to them.

Sometimes when we experience unwanted encounters or emotions, our initial reaction is to disown it. Either it's too painful, we don't have the emotional tools to cope with it, or it challenges our self-identity, so we push it down to keep going on with business as usual. But what we reject stays with us; it becomes our shadow, and our shadow can have very real-life implications. We first addressed our shadow in chapter 4 with Main Character Energy, and now we will explore shadow work as it relates to family dynamics. The shadow, a term coined by psychologist Carl Jung, refers to the dark side of our consciousness. He described it as "the thing a person has no wish to be."[1] Essentially, our shadow is the part of ourselves we don't want to identify with and, therefore, the part of ourselves that we want to separate ourselves from. Many women, especially Black women, find that we are labeled as angry, when deep down we are really hurt. But when we express our pain, many times we are dismissed, rejected, and even vilified. I, like many women, attempted to cover my hurt with anger for many years because I became ashamed of it. Maybe you were a naturally creative child but were told to be serious, so as an adult you hide that part of yourself. Maybe you have alternative beliefs that you hide for fear of being ostracized. Whatever the case may be, many of us are guilty of internalizing shame about who we truly are.

The process of distancing ourselves from aspects of who we are is a form of emotional repression, which psychological studies have shown can lead to a higher chance of depression, anxiety, and even a weakened immune system.[2] In my case, I discovered as an adult that chronic and prolonged stress had caused my adrenals to become fatigued, which had a domino effect, dysregulating other hormones in my body. You cannot hone Main Character Energy or deconstruct your Crooked

Room if you haven't done some form of inner child work. Naturally, you are human and may engage in varying degrees of repression, consciously or unconsciously, and that's okay. The goal is not perfection; it's to do the best you can with the information available at every step.

In this chapter, we'll get in touch with our child self so we can get to the root of some of our deepest struggles and unearth the emotions we have pushed away. I don't want to sugarcoat it—this is tough work. But it's so rewarding when you're able to gradually peel away the layers that keep your heart's truth buried away and freely express yourself in all ways without fear, shame, or guilt.

GENERATIONAL ANXIETIES

"I'm having trouble staying asleep through the night," I remember telling my therapist. "I just don't know why I'm so anxious. Sometimes I feel like I'm about to fall off a cliff, but everything is fine. Or sometimes I fall asleep, but then I'm up wide awake in a few hours." I could feel my body getting hot and my breath quickening.

"Have you ever heard of epigenetics?" my therapist asked.

"No, what's that?"

"Let me explain it this way. When a female fetus is in the womb, she already has all the cells that will later specialize into other cells. So when your grandmother was pregnant with your mother, you were technically in her womb also."

"Wait, what?"

"Mhm. So let's say your grandmother also had anxiety, right? You had that experience in *her* womb, and then you experienced anxiety in your mother's body throughout her life, including when you were in utero. And then this experience was further reinforced by watching your mother experience anxiety throughout your childhood."

I sat quietly, feeling a confusing mixture of relief and sadness. Sadness about my grandmother's and mother's experience and relief that maybe there wasn't something just fundamentally wrong with me.

What my therapist was talking about in our session can also be described as *generational anxiety*. According to psychiatrist Dr. Bruce Perry, we pass information on to our children through lived experiences, genetics (DNA), and epigenetics. Epigenetics refers to modifying and controlling gene expression by turning specific genetic markers on or off. In fact, Dr. Perry says that every cell in your body has the same genes, but not every cell has the same genes "turned on."[3] For example, in the famous "Cherry Blossom Experiment," researchers taught male mice to fear the smell of cherry blossoms by associating the scent with mild foot shocks. Two weeks later, they allowed the mice to breed with females. The resulting pups were raised to adulthood having never been exposed to the cherry blossom smell, yet when they caught a whiff of it for the first time, the pups suddenly became anxious and fearful.[4]

This new insight made me question if every single one of my "worry about everything all the time" genes was turned on. My mother was forced to figure out life largely by herself, without the support of her family, and without knowing, I had learned to do the same. One recurring topic for me in my own journey was feeling like I was parentified so young, feeling like I was always an adult with responsibilities that I had neither the preparedness or readiness for.

My supreme goal for Unruly women is freedom—the freedom to choose how you show up, what stories you tell yourself about your life, and when you can finally let go of what no longer serves you. The harm some of us experienced as children did not start with us, but it can end with us. Harm can look like feeling ignored, not being supported when needed, witnessing your parents fight, living through food or money insecurity, favoritism among siblings, moving to a new city or school, or physical and/or emotional abuse.

Harm does not always point to bad intentions or poor parenting. Say, for example, your mom or dad got a new job, which caused the whole family to relocate to a different state. If moving meant leaving the school you loved, this may have caused you some level of harm or trauma. Your parents could have been making the best decision for the family, and you could still have been really hurt to leave your friends at school. Many things can be true at the same time.

Unfortunately, some of you may have endured unspeakable traumas that you are not ready to face, and that's okay. Start from where you are and move forward as you can, or if you can, reach out for more support from a professional.

If you went through your entire childhood without any perceived harm from your parents, use these exercises to give gratitude and spend some time honoring your inner child regardless. I won't sell you the idea that inner child healing is a one-size-fits-all solution or that you will magically heal all forms of childhood trauma. But I have seen incredible healing transformations, and I intend for the following meditations to provide the same for you. In its essence, inner child work frees you from continuing to react from the place of a child. From acting out old stories. If you go through life in this way, you'll never experience the gift of being present, and instead you will perform the past indefinitely. Again, I want you to be able to choose how you show up.

By looking closely at your childhood patterns, you get the opportunity to see the origins of some of your behaviors, whether desired or undesired. You open yourself up to a deeper level of freedom when you heal the child within you, who may not have had the opportunity or skills to process their emotions effectively. You can do that for your younger self now.

SPEND TIME WITH LITTLE YOU

Now that you understand how important inner child work is for your healing journey, it's time to cultivate that relationship with little you. While what may come up could be pretty serious and possibly traumatic, our work with our little me doesn't have to be stuffy and sad all the time. It can be fun, silly, eye-opening, nourishing, or even relaxing. Try out the following exercises when you need a little pick-me-up.

When You Need Some Fun

Find a picture of your younger self and settle into a quiet room. Look into your younger self's eyes in the image and try to put yourself back in that moment. If you don't have access to a photo, use your mind's eye to think back to a time when you were younger. In your journal, list the things she liked to do for fun. What did she enjoy doing that made her feel safe and happy? What brought her joy, made her laugh, settled her nerves? Once you have your list, choose one activity to do within the next forty-eight hours and take note of how you feel. Know that just by doing this simple act, you are beginning to heal your little self's heart.

When You Need a Hug

Complete this meditation anytime you are feeling difficult or painful emotions in the present. Your intention for this meditation is to provide care and comfort to a younger version of you who needed it.

Sit or lie in a comfortable position. Take a few deep breaths and relax. Don't try to do anything or make anything happen; simply be in this moment. When you're settled, gently place your hand over your heart and imagine your breath coming directly from your heart's center with each inhale. Take a few deep, comforting breaths.

If any negative self-talk or thoughts attempt to distract you, gently guide yourself back to this caring, kind heart feeling, the same way you would guide a small child, and connect with the unwanted feelings.

Take a moment to visualize your younger self standing in a room with adult you. Gently bring her in for a hug. Let her feel safe and handled warmly. Stay in this space of togetherness for as long as you'd like. Be open to the reality that whatever energy you give to her will be returned to your adult self. Accept and allow that both of you are receiving deep, freeing healing. Take a moment to sit with this knowing. When you're ready, slowly open your eyes and return to the present.

When You Want to Give/Receive a Gift
Complete this meditation whenever you feel your needs are not being met. Your intention for this meditation is to give a younger version of yourself something that they needed but did not get, which in turn will energetically give yourself something in return.

Find yourself in a comfortable position. Take a deep breath in and out without trying to make anything special happen. Bring your attention to the natural rhythm of your breath rising and falling. Bring your attention to your heart and imagine you are breathing directly from your heart's center. Allow yourself to feel a sense of tender care and love for yourself. Allow this feeling to expand from your heart, throughout your chest, to your arms, legs, neck, and head until your entire body is covered in this loving, kind energy emanating from your heart.

If any negative self-talk attempts to distract you during this meditation, just think of this caring, kind feeling and gently guide yourself back to the meditation the same way you would guide a small child.

Imagine yourself walking through a toy store, browsing casually. Out of the corner of your eye, you notice a small child walking around the store too, picking up toys with a slight smile and then moving on to the next. As she gets closer, you realize that she is a younger version of you. Pause here and take note of as much detail as possible. What kind of clothes is she wearing? How old is she?

She says she has a gift for you and playfully runs off. She returns with a big white box with a pretty gold ribbon and proudly extends the box out in front of you. As you take the box, you become filled with anticipation and excitement. What would you like to receive? What do you need right now? What do you want to be in that box? Now, open the box. What's in it?

You decide to return the favor by giving her exactly what you know she wants. Suddenly another beautifully wrapped gift with gold ribbon appears on the shelf next to you. When you give it to her, her face lights up with joy. She squeals as she grabs your waist to hug you. Both of you take a moment to revel in this selfless joy and each other's company, but soon you realize it's time to go.

You thank her again for the gift and start to part ways. Right before you exit the store, she says she wants to tell you something. Allow her to say one simple phrase to you. What is it? And with that, she happily runs off.

As you leave the store, you feel a weight has been lifted because your younger self supplied you with everything you needed. You realize that all the answers, wisdom, love, and joy you desire already live within you, and if you ever need a pick-me-up, you have a little person here to remind you.

Unruly Unquiry

What gifts did you give each other? Why did you both choose those particular gifts? What did she have to say to you? How did her message make you feel?

Inner child healing opens you up to profound healing and growth, so as you continue to walk this path of inner growth, do not forget the child within you that accompanies you every step of the way. Sometimes, when you're having an irrational emotional experience in the present, it's helpful to consider that it may be a younger you simply vying for your attention. Now that we've done inner child work, you are in the perfect position to think more deeply about how you actively perform who you are. In the next chapter, I'll share what my acting training taught me about how we are always performing, whether we know it or not, and how we can use this to our benefit.

**Repeat after me: I have everything I need
to care for and protect myself.**

8

Presence Over Presenting

"Acting is behaving truthfully under
imaginary circumstances."

– Sanford Meisner[1]

The term "manifesting" as we know it today refers to the idea that thoughts become things. Your thoughts are the building blocks of your reality, because what you think about will dictate your actions, which will dictate your reality. If you want to change your reality, you must change your thoughts. I have seen this concept work miracles in my life. I manifested my company Curvy, Curly, Conscious and my marriage. They started as thoughts in my mind. They were once vague visualizations in meditations and journaling pages—and now they are a part of my everyday life. In this chapter, I will go into my favorite manifestation technique—but first, let's explore some common manifestation myths.

MANIFESTATION MYTH #1: JUST THINK ABOUT IT, AND YOU CAN HAVE IT.

Just think of the dream job you want, and then it appears. Just visualize the money you want, and it will come. Not exactly. Holding the reality you desire in your mind is a critical part of the manifestation process, but it's not the *only* step in the process. Over-emphasis on thoughts ignores any necessary actions that you need to take. There will likely be day-to-day hard work that goes into achieving the things that you want. Visualizing and hard work are not mutually exclusive; faith without works is dead. Visualizing allows you to get clear on the type of work you should be doing that will actually get you closer to your goal—so instead of spinning your wheels, just being busy, you are actually funneling your energy toward that which you desire. Adjusting your thoughts is the first step, but there are more after that.

MANIFESTATION MYTH #2: YOU ATTRACT WHAT YOU WANT.

Another huge manifesting myth is that you attract what you want. The truth is you attract what you *are*. Your presence becomes the present. The trick is not chasing what you want, but instead practicing *being* the thing that you want. Practice makes reality. This shifts your focus from wanting, wishing, and hoping to embodying and performing your desires. I would argue that the most important takeaway from this chapter is the skill to *be* what you want instead of chasing what you want. Because if you do, you will have what you desire because you are it—regardless of what it looks like on the outside.

MANIFESTATION MYTH #3: THERE'S NO CROOKED ROOM.

I'll never forget when one of my friends in college came home raving about this new book: Rhonda Byrne's *The Secret*. I was immediately intrigued, like "What's the secret? I want to know!" I found the DVD version at Strozier Library on FSU's campus and watched it in full that night. I distinctly remember the part of the film where this man talked about how he manifested a parking spot. He said all he had to do was imagine the spot and then it would appear. *Hell yeah*, I thought. I was tired of being late to class because the parking garage was full. I was tired of feeling out of control and powerless in my life and not feeling like I had the skills or the ability to curate my reality in the way I wanted.

There's a reason why this concept is very appealing to people who live in an individualistic society like America. We are conditioned to think that all of our successes come uniquely from us, and all of our failures also come uniquely from us. We have less of a grasp on the idea of "collective consciousness" or the ways in which perceived failures and successes are interwoven with those of the people around us. And as a millennial, part of one of the potentially loneliest generations to ever live, the idea that I, all by myself, could change my life was something that I wanted to access when I first started my healing journey. For better or worse, I felt solely responsible for my future.

Books like *The Secret* teach simply that if you can think it, you can create it. And if you want it and don't have it, you have to change your thoughts to get it. The big problem I have with this brand of New Age manifestation doctrine, or the idea that your reality is a direct byproduct of your thoughts, is that it is ahistorical, apolitical, and acontextual. *You* need to change your thoughts. *You* need to change your energetic vibration, so your reality can mirror that. It neglects The Crooked Room. You are very much manifesting in a Crooked Room, and acknowledging that is imperative.

Anything can be weaponized in search of power, especially spiritual concepts. They sometimes float above reproach or critical inspection, and I think the "thoughts become things" concept can, in some instances, be an insidious way of justifying the privilege of certain groups and the harms they perpetuate. Yes, your thoughts do become things. But telling marginalized groups or survivors of trauma that everything in their life is happening because of their thoughts can get very close to victim blaming, and there is no healing in that dynamic. This can also embolden people who have money, power, and visibility to automatically assume they are deserving of everything they have because of some divine law, ignoring the unearned privilege, unfair advantages, and sometimes even ruthless exploitation that takes places in pursuit of their goals. In addition to ignoring The Crooked Room, this myth also over-prioritizes the spiritual law of attraction. The law of attraction is just one spiritual law, not the only law. And spiritual principles are all interconnected and can show up in our lives in complex ways. Magnetizing the life you desire is a product of your thoughts, but shifting your thoughts does not mean you can override karmic patterns or soul lessons.

MANIFESTING MYTH #4: YOU ARE THE SUM OF WHAT YOU MANIFEST.

The rest of this chapter will focus on how to manifest, but please keep this in mind: you are not the sum of what you produce. You are not your clean house, well-mannered children, monthly salary, or social media likes. Dismantle the idea that your output determines your worth. You are not what you produce. Abandon the notion that you have to do anything at all to be worthy. You are worthy because you are human. You don't have to earn your seat at the table through demonstrating that you are valuable. You already are, just sit. Abandon the notion that you must do anything or possess something to be worthy of your desires. You are worthy simply because you exist.

A PINTEREST-WORTHY PRESENTATION

I was super obsessed with manifesting going into 2019. I was going to reach all the goals and do all the things. So, I did what many people do when they want to manifest something. I made a dream board on Pinterest, which went something like this:

Title: Manifestation 2019

- A picture of a group of smiling women in bathing suits on a boat (I wanted to produce another successful Unruly Retreat).

- A picture of a person giving a speech to a crowd (I wanted to be booked on more panel discussions and speaking gigs).

- A picture of a dramatic entry to a home with hardwood flooring, natural light, and high ceilings (I wanted my husband and me to have our first dream home).

I was going to be a manifesting queen; or so I thought. 2019 was the busiest year ever for my company Curvy, Curly, Conscious (CCC). On our company calendar we had a national tour of our signature Playshop events (a day of fun, play, and healing for women); an online meditation circle; a series of webinars; scheduled long-form YouTube content for my personal channel; short-form Instagram content for both myself and CCC; and our first-ever retreat. I was in the midst of organically building a profitable brand on social media, producing sold-out events, and building a community. But despite it all, I did not *feel* successful. I had everything I wanted on paper, so why didn't that period feel fulfilling? Because I was over-prioritizing the aesthetics and not considering the emotional experience required to *feel* those aesthetics.

Behind the image of smiling women at a retreat was meeting payroll for three employees and not having enough to pay myself. Behind the picture of a person speaking to an audience were hours and hours of headache-inducing business meetings with spreadsheets and projections with super-smart Excel formulas. Behind the image of success was the reality of being a CEO: Putting out one fire after another. Constantly checking notifications from text messages, Voxer, Calendly, Asana, Slack, Google Docs, and a host of other project management tools. Ironically, behind the Pinterest board was this intense feeling of not being good enough. I was utterly tone-deaf to my inner voice, muting what my honest wants and needs were at the time, all to get the look right.

I was prioritizing the presentation over presence. In pursuit of being an aesthetics queen, we risk betraying ourselves. If we are overly married to a specific image and not listening to the inner voice that's trying to tell us something is off, we're going to be onstage giving a performance that might please an audience, but leaves us feeling unfulfilled. You are not manifesting a social media feed; you are creating a life that complements your emotional needs and desires. The most critical element of manifesting is intimate communication with yourself about your emotional life. You are not here just for vibes and aesthetics alone. You're here for vibes and aesthetics *and* the emotional experience of your deepest desires.

USING YOUR PRESENCE TO CREATE THE PRESENT

Seasoned performers don't perform *for* an audience, they perform authentically *in front* of one. And whether you realize it or not, we are always performing ourselves. Remember, you are not seeking to *get* something; instead, you are seeking to *be* something. You are what you attract. What you focus on magnifies, and what you desire already desires you. Using this logic, the following manifesting method is a quick process you can use to fast-track your desires through a bit of reverse engineering.

Step One: Name the Desire

In your journal, start by naming what you want. For example, in 2019, one of my goals was to produce a sold-out, international retreat that was a safe space for women of color. (At that time, I was producing retreats for all women of color, I hadn't yet narrowed it down to just Black women.) Make sure to be specific here so you will know exactly when you have achieved your goal. Sometimes, we are living in an answered prayer and don't even know it. The more specific you get about what you seek, the more likely you will be to actually recognize it when you accomplish it. One of the most significant goal killers is vagueness and non-specificity.

Step Two: Experience the Desire

Now that you have your goal clearly defined, take a moment to imagine what your life would be like if you were living in that reality. How do you feel in your body when you imagine yourself achieving your desired outcome? Pay special attention to the **three predominant feelings** you feel while you are imagining yourself. Noting your feelings is important for our next step. Common feelings that ladies have noted during this exercise include:

I feel...

Admired	Joyful
Appreciated	Content
Fulfilled	Peaceful
Energized	Hopeful
Powerful	Calm
Confident	Safe
Strong	

I feel

_____,

_____, and

_____.

Step Three: Create Your Emotional Algorithm

The word "algorithm" is a part of the popular consciousness now that we have social media. Social media platforms create algorithms, or equations, that curate content in a way to keep users engaged. For example, if you interact with foodie content, the algorithm will learn this about you and show you more food-related posts. Social media algorithms learn your interests and then reflect them back to you. In the same way you can adjust your social media feed by being selective about what you engage with, you are going to create your own Emotional Algorithm to train yourself to expect these emotional states. The three emotions I wrote down were:

I feel confident, powerful, and accomplished.

These three emotions will now serve as your Emotional Algorithm. You see, the problem with how we typically approach our goals is that we want to feel a certain way, and we use our goals as placeholders for those feelings. Instead, the three emotions you named as your Emotional Algorithm can serve as your guide for your goal. The more you engage with your Emotional Algorithm, the more these emotions will show up for you in your daily life. In this way, your Emotional Algorithm allows you to cut out the middleman of a goal and get what you deeply desire (your Emotional Algorithm) with more ease.

Place the actual goal to the side for now. Instead, your job is to condition yourself to feel these emotions without needing to have achieved a particular goal. It's a win-win; you release pressure on yourself and end up with the emotional experience you were looking for, regardless of the outcome of your goal. In 2019, I made the mistake of thinking that the goal would bring me my Emotional Algorithm and ended up having the exact opposite emotional experience. I felt pressured, insecure, and not-enough. I've since learned that goals are great to have, but the real destination should be our Emotional Algorithm. Here are some exercises you can do to practice embodying your Emotional Algorithm.

Emotional Algorithm Exercises

MUSCLE MEMORY

Write your Emotional Algorithm down on sticky notes, with one word per sticky note. Practice saying each one out loud throughout the day. As you focus on the word, imagine the feeling surging through your body. Remind yourself of these words often by keeping them as the screensaver on your phone, in your car, in your journal, etc. Anywhere that you can remind yourself often to practice feeling these feelings. This might seem like an elementary activity, but think of this as building muscle. The more you practice this, the more effective you'll be at it, and the outcome is supremely gratifying.

IFFIRMATIONS

I first learned the term "Iffirmation" on social media from a post made by Christy Gibson, MD. She stated that sometimes affirmations don't feel authentic because we don't fully believe them.[2] Typically, affirmations require that you state your desire in a short, present-tense statement, like "I am successful." The concept of an iffirmation flips this on its head by posing the phrase as a question for your subconscious to answer: "What if I already am successful?" Using this technique, you can turn your Emotional Algorithm into iffirmations:

What if I am already powerful?

What if I am already confident?

What if I am already accomplished?

Put your iffirmations on sticky notes and use them like you did in the previous exercise.

RECORD IT
Turn your iffirmation into your own personal meditation track. Use the voice note feature on your phone or any recording device to record yourself saying your iffirmations. You can play this track in the car, in the background while multitasking, and even while you sleep.

JUSTIFY IT
There's a possibility that what you want is right in front of you, and you just haven't given specific attention to it. Sometimes being goal-oriented can make us feel like we are never where we want to be. This can make us insatiable in our pursuit of the next big thing, like a higher-ranking job, more money, a bigger house, a better body, a newer car, and so on. Justifying your iffirmations places you in a state of gratitude for where you are and all you currently have. For each emotion, provide a justification for how or why you already feel it: "I am already [insert emotion] because [insert reason]."

Examples
> I am already confident because I connect with my audience in a vulnerable, genuine way.

> I am already powerful because I have a community that trusts me.
>
> I am already accomplished because I am a published author.

Hopefully, by this point, you feel more clear about exactly what you desire, and you have the confidence in yourself to reach for it and turn your dreams into real-life actions. If you're not quite there just yet, that's OK! Continue to speak positivity into yourself and your journey, and come back to this exercise when you feel you need a reminder of who you are and what you want.

....

NOT YOUR EVERYDAY MANIFESTATION HACK: MASTURBATION AND MANIFESTATION

There's absolutely no way I could finish the topic of manifestation without sharing one of my absolute favorite workshops I've ever done, alongside sexual therapist and educator Samia Burton. She shared a unique method that harnesses pleasure as a tool for manifesting. This can be a controversial technique, and this section involves talk of self-pleasure in a very unapologetic and candid way, so if that is not your thing, feel free to move on to the next chapter.

I will summarize Samia's teachings with our group and share her top manifestation and masturbation tips—I'll call them *Touch Points*.

Touch Point #1: Treat Yourself

Samia shared that when most women settle in for a self-pleasure session, they cheat themselves out of a full experience.

Many women may only be able to steal a few minutes alone, so we rush into the room, lock the door, and get the job done as soon as possible. When you can, Samia told us to take our time. Set the scene, light a candle, dim the lights, and try to give yourself at least 15 minutes. Research shows that women take at least that long to become fully roused.

Touch Point #2: Talk Nice & Nasty

Samia shared that we record ourselves talking *nice* and *nasty* to ourselves about our goals and play it while we masturbate. Nice = giving yourself a compliment. Nasty = sexy self-talk. This blend of affirmation and pleasure sends the message to yourself that you are worthy and deserving of pleasure. You are to give yourself compliments, in a nasty way, speaking positive, present-tense, naughty statements. This method of manifestation works by linking the achievement of our goals to a reliable feeling of satisfaction. You're teaching yourself that your ability to feel good aids you in pursuing your desires. I know, I know! I was equal parts uncomfortable and wildly intrigued the first time she shared this information with me.

If you're interested in giving this a try, you can incorporate this method into your next self-pleasure session. You just record yourself and then play it back while you pleasure yourself. Here's an example from Samia: "You know what? You did so great today in your workout, baby. You so deserve to cum. Look at what you did. Look how amazing you look. Look at you following that healthy diet. You're so dedicated. You're so resilient. I'm so proud of you. You are doing your thing, girl."

Touch Point #3: Reward and Repeat

Every time you need to take a step in your manifestation journey that requires a lot of labor, make sure you accompany that with a self-pleasure session, then follow it up with another self-pleasure session after you've taken action. In the beginning, you will use your self-pleasure time to achieve the desired outcome. But eventually, you'll be in a cycle where you also reward yourself after achieving a goal by masturbating. It's going to be a never-ending cycle of self-pleasure. You are going to use self-pleasure to motivate yourself *and* reward yourself. You give yourself permission to enjoy working toward a particular goal and give yourself much-needed acknowledgment for your labor. It's so profound and healing for a woman to be rewarding herself, telling herself how well she's doing, and giving herself an orgasm at the same time.

Of all the transformation practices I've learned, this is by far the most enjoyable to practice. I've become more acquainted with my body and given myself some much-needed care and attention. Samia has so many more practices that nurture sexual fulfillment and liberation; please visit her website, sexualessentials.com, to stay updated on what she has coming up next.

Congrats! You are officially a manifesting goddess, or you're on your way at least. I hope you were able to add some new tools to your Unruly tool kit to support your expansion and growth. To stay in line with manifestation, I want to stretch your dreaming ability even more, so in the next chapter, we will explore one of my favorite manifesting tools: Serious Daydreaming. This mind-bending tool will help nurture your curiosity about who you are today and open your mind to all the possible versions of who you could become.

9

What's Your Next Scene?

Serious Daydreaming

I open my eyes to bright sunlight pouring into my bedroom. My husband is asleep next to me with his arm draped over my stomach, his waist-length locs beautifully piled up on his pillow. There's no alarm to abruptly pull us from our slumber because we are both self-employed. I am a writer and an event producer, and he is some kind of creative. A writer? An artist? Maybe a musician? He looks like he could be an athlete, but I know that's not his profession. I get up to make breakfast—something healthy, light, and satisfying—before I start my day.

Suddenly, my phone's timer sounded.

I opened my eyes, adjusted to my current reality, and remembered that I was single, working as a teaching artist, I didn't own a home, and I did have to get up with an alarm clock. I slowly felt this pervasive, nagging sadness creep back into my mind and body as I settled back in the bedroom of my Brooklyn apartment. I'd agreed to try a quantum meditation session my friend recommended from the book *Quantum Jumping* by Burt Goldman. The book was a little far out for me, but I was unhappy, committed to healing, and willing to try almost anything.

One of the techniques in the book was based on the idea that there are unlimited parallel universes with unlimited versions of yourself, all existing right now simultaneously. So if you are lacking something in this reality, you could just borrow it from one of your other unlimited selves. Years ago, I was watching an IMAX movie about a group of NASA astronauts. Throughout the film, we got to see how they worked and lived, but the last few minutes of footage stuck with me years after seeing it. The space team discovered a planet almost the same size as Earth at a similar distance from its sun, meaning it had the potential to sustain life. Scientists call this The Goldilocks Zone.[1] Not too close and not too far. Just right for life to exist. The film ended by reminding us of our infinite universe, which contains billions of galaxies. Read that again: not billions of stars or planets or solar systems—but billions of *galaxies*. We live on one tiny planet in one solar system in one galaxy in an ever-expanding universe that is home to billions of galaxies. Who knows what's out there, and who can say what is and isn't possible for you?

I won't definitively claim, as *Quantum Jumping* does, that you have twin selves just chilling on other planets, but I can vouch for the effectiveness of this practice when you allow yourself to get into it. Unruly women are trailblazers and explorers. Unruly women question what's beyond the everyday. Being Unruly requires indulging in your imagination. You don't have the luxury of copying what's been done before you, so Serious Daydreaming will be an essential tool for you to see new possibilities for yourself and get to know yourself more intimately. When else do you get to dream and test the limits of your imagination? Serious Daydreaming is a time for you to expand your muscle for creative problem-solving and get clear on what your next big scene is.

There I was, in my midtwenties, freshly heartbroken, and at the start of my healing journey. I desperately wanted to be partnered with a man. I had judged this desire for years and was finally starting to let this self-described shameful truth bubble to the surface. My truth was I desired a mate, a best friend, someone to grow deeply with. At the time, I was losing fantastically at the love game in my third-dimensional reality, so I decided to play with the idea of meeting an alternate version of myself who did have the luck: happily married Shelah. What did I have to lose? I had already used all my free therapy sessions at NYU, so I tried almost anything to cope with the bouts of depression and anxiety that always seemed to sneak up on me. What I didn't know then was that this simple meditation session would turn out to be one of my most potent tools for transformation.

Since that day, I have spent countless hours honing my own version of quantum meditation individually and with my community. Those early meditation sessions eventually evolved into Serious Daydreaming, a visualization practice I developed where you connect with an alternate version of yourself, your Sister-Self, to gain insight, clarity, or direction. Think of your Sister-Self as your faithful companion, best friend, advice-giver, your higher self, your intuition, and anything else you need her to be. She's your all-knowing sidekick. If you can't, she can. If you don't know, she does.

The Serious Daydreaming method is "serious" because you can use it to tangibly change the course of your life. A great example is a story from one of our Unruly ladies during our last retreat. We had just completed a Serious Daydreaming session, and the group was journaling their experience. I noticed someone, who I'll call Jenn, silently crying with her head in her hands. In between crying, Jenn whispered to me that she had just found out she was six weeks pregnant the night before, and she was devastated. She explained that she saw her Sister-Self living in a house in a sunny climate with three children, the third being a cute little girl in a high chair. At the time, she lived in Washington, DC, and only had two kids. She didn't understand what she saw during her daydream session. Not only had she not been to any doctor appointments or gotten any gender testing done, but she wasn't even sure if she would keep the baby. Between sobs, she told me that she wasn't confident that she and her partner could care for another child. She just kept saying, "But I felt her."

After the retreat, I kept in touch with her, and she told me, "Those Serious Daydreaming sessions are the only reason my youngest baby is here." She didn't just *see* a different life for herself but she *felt* it, and she was led by that feeling. She didn't have to make complete sense of the vision; she just had to trust what she felt during the meditation. She followed that feeling, one step at a time, toward the reality of her Sister-Self. Since then, she has relocated from Washington, DC, to Florida with her family, including her now two-year-old daughter.

Remember the vision I shared at the start of the chapter? Well, that session was one of many. I was so disillusioned with my dating life that I would visit my Sister-Self as much as possible—before work, on the train to work, after work. Sometimes I did three sessions in one day. But what I was really doing was training myself to recognize an emotional state in my body. When I spent time with my Sister-Self and her husband, I felt this warm, safe, kinetic energy.

I still casually dated, hoping to feel that feeling with someone outside of meditation, but with no luck. Soon after, though, because I had conditioned myself to spend so much time in that feeling, it finally found me in my "real" life. It started with an inconspicuous heart emoji on one of my pictures on Instagram. I thought there was no way a platinum-selling, world-famous recording artist would have found my Instagram account. I was sure I was being catfished. That was until the first time I saw him, and I felt that feeling I had grown to know so well. I didn't know the next steps or how we would be together with his schedule, my work, and living in two separate states, but I knew I had to follow that feeling.

As I write this, I am sitting in my home office with sunlight pouring in. I did not wake up to an alarm today; many days I don't, because we both are self-employed. After a slow, quiet breakfast, I received an email from my team confirming that we have sold out the 2023 Unruly Retreat. The version of myself I am now would not be possible without the relationship I cultivated with my Sister-Self all those years ago.

THE SERIOUS DAYDREAMING METHOD
Step One: Find Stillness

Dropping into a Serious Daydreaming practice is about expansion, imagination, and possibility. This is not the place for your logical brain to run the show; she already does that enough in your daily life. Revisit the Judgmental Brain Dump activity in chapter 1 if you need to. First, you'll need to get centered and quiet the doubting inner voice that will attempt to keep you "rational." Western ideologies have convinced us that our primary sense of knowing comes from logic, reason, and evidence. If you can't prove it, it doesn't exist. But in reality, we live in a world where things happen all the time that cannot be explained. Stonehenge, the pyramids in Egypt, the paranormal, daylight savings time (I kid, I kid). The point I'm making is you've already tried the rational/logical approach, so now, I invite you to open yourself up to the possibility of something new. Abandon the idea of being "right." You do not have to be right, or accurate, or practical right now; you just have to be open. Open to new solutions, new ideas, and new suggestions that you already have within you.

In this step, your goal is to become very still and centered so you can supersede the monkey brain, or our mind's tendency to be distracted and scattered. My favorite way to do this is through meditation and breathwork. You can use any of your favorite breathing techniques or the ones I share here to raise your vibration to the level of your Sister-Self.

If breathwork and meditation are not accessible for you, you can go on a nature walk, a meditative walk, or use any other technique that will allow you to get deeply centered. However you do it, it's important that you get as centered as possible because without this step the rest of the process will not be effective.

You'll know you're centered by the way you feel in your body: tingling sensations, a feeling of being lighter, or an overall sense of calmness and quiet are most common. You may also notice your senses becoming heightened, and your thoughts may begin to shift to being more observatory, like you're listening to yourself or watching yourself from within.

Breathing Techniques
In and Out Breath: For this breathwork exercise, begin by breathing in through your nose. Once your lungs are comfortably filled, hold this breath for a few seconds, release it through your mouth, then hold again. It's important to note that you should

not breathe fully in or fully out. This is a controlled breath. Repeat this breathing cycle at least four times.

4-7-8 Breath: This breathing technique was developed by Dr. Andrew Weil, a renowned integrative medicine physician. It's fairly simple to do and can be completed anywhere and any time you need to settle your nervous system.

1. Place the tip of your tongue against the ridge of tissue just behind your upper front teeth. Keep it there throughout the exercise.

2. Exhale completely through your mouth, making a whooshing sound.

3. Close your mouth and inhale silently through your nose to a mental count of four.

4. Hold your breath for a count of seven.

5. Exhale completely through your mouth, making a whooshing sound, to a count of eight. This completes one breath. Repeat the cycle three more times for a total of four breaths.[2]

Step Two: Set Your Intention

This is where Serious Daydreaming departs from other meditation practices. Having a specific goal in mind for your session can be antithetical to many mindfulness practices that aim to move you beyond attachment to expectations. I encourage you to keep mindfulness meditation as a part of your daily practice, but think of Serious Daydreaming as a tool you can use when you need it. The method works best when you identify a specific need you would like to meet before starting. In my case, I wanted to feel what it would be like to be married. In the case of my student, she wanted guidance on her new pregnancy. You can use this technique to get information about *anything*. Don't know what to write next? Ask your Sister-Self. Nervous about having a conversation? Go ask your Sister-Self about it. Unsure about accepting that project? Go see what your Sister-Self thinks. Literally anything.

Step Three: Meet Your Sister-Self

When you've settled into the calmness of your daydream session, prepare to enter your Sister-Self's reality. I use the imagery of a door to conceptualize leaving this reality and entering another. You are going to imagine yourself leaving your present reality, going through a door, and entering the life of your Sister-Self. When you enter, assume the role of an omniscient visitor and pick up on as much detail as possible. Pay attention to *everything*. Take note of any sounds, smells, emotions, people, or things that stand out to you.

Step Four: Take Notes

Do not skip this step. After a meditation, take a few minutes to take notes. How did it go? What worked? What didn't? Note anything you saw, anything that made you pause, any feelings you experienced, and any messages you may have received. Some things don't make sense right now, but they can down the line. It's useful to have this documentation to refer back to. Also, mundane tweaks can have major changes in our life, so something as small as what your Sister-Self eats or what time she goes to bed could be valuable information for you.

BEGINNER SERIOUS DAYDREAMING EXERCISES
Day in the Life of Your Sister-Self

Close your eyes and imagine yourself standing in front of a large door. You know that your Sister-Self is on the other side of that door. She is expecting you, and you know you will meet her when you open the door. On the count of three, open the door and enter your Sister-Self's home. 1, 2, 3.

It's morning and your Sister-Self is going about her routine as normal. Pay attention to every detail you can pick up. Does she live alone? With a partner? Are there children there? Can you name what city she's in? Is it an apartment? A home? A condo? Take notice of her clothes. Does she work? If so, where? What does she do? What kind of car does she drive? Does she walk or bike to work instead? Time passes so fast in this beautiful life. It's already midday. What happens now? Does she eat lunch? Is her workday finished? Again, take note of all the details she shares with you, no matter how small.

It's evening now, the sun is setting, signaling the transition from day to night. It's almost time for your Sister-Self to lie down for a night of peaceful sleep. What's her nighttime routine? How does she wind down and get ready for bed? Before you go, take some time to feel the energy of the space. In this moment, you notice that the only difference between you and your Sister-Self is the vibration she holds. If you choose, you can have it too by merging with her and taking that vibration with you outside of the meditation and into your life.

Face your Sister-Self and move closer to her as the energy emanating from her intensifies. It feels electric. This is the energy that helps her magnetize her desires. Stand toe to toe with your Sister-Self and merge with her on the count of three. 1, 2, 3.

Now you are ready to go, and you are prepared to take this light with you. Say thank you to your Sister-Self for spending time with you and find the door you entered through at the beginning of this meditation. When you are ready, exit the door.

Hone Your Focus

Find yourself in a comfortable position in a quiet, private space. For this practice, your eyes will remain open. Sit about eight to ten feet away from a wall. Choose a small spot on the wall, about the size of a fingernail. Hold a soft gaze on that spot. Send all of your focus to just that spot. Practice honing your focus so much that you don't see anything else in the room but that spot.

Now, keep that spot in the center of your vision while also widening your frame of reference at the same time. Start with just that spot and now see if you can widen your field of vision by about one foot in diameter on all sides of that spot.

Now, widen your field of vision to include about three feet in diameter around that spot. Now, widen your field of vision to include about six feet in diameter with your spot in the center.

Now, see if you can keep your focus on that initial spot in the center of your field of vision while taking in the entire room at the same time. Practice focusing on your initial small spot and taking in detail all around you at the same time.

Practice Your Visualization Skills

Level 1: Find yourself in a quiet, private space. For this exercise, your eyes will remain open. Look around the room and take in as much detail as you can. Start with the things near you, and keep widening your field of vision until you have taken in as much detail as you can in the entire room you're sitting in.

Give yourself about three minutes to do this. Think of it like you are visually memorizing the room.

Now, close your eyes. Practice building the room in your mind's eye from your memory. See how much detail you can remember. You can come back to this practice as many times as you want. You can open your eyes and see how well you've done, and then go back and close your eyes and try again. This is a practice exercise, so make it work for you.

Level 2: For a more advanced step in this practice exercise, memorize the room that you're in, close your eyes and re-create the space, but this time with one small change. So, create the room that you're in right now to the best of your ability, but with one small change that you make in your mind's eye.

MORE ADVANCED SERIOUS DAYDREAMING EXERCISES

- Replay old scenarios with a new ending and take that energy with you.

- Ask your Sister-Self for advice via a simple, one-sentence question. Examples: Would you take this job? Should I accept that offer? Should I stay in this relationship?

- Hang out with her with no other objective. Just spend time with her and enjoy yourself.

- Visit your Sister-Self one year from today.

I can't wait for you to discover who you can become through the power of imagination and dreaming. Have fun practicing Serious Daydreaming in your life, and keep striving to allow yourself more and more permission to trust your innate creative power and vision.

We've spent the last few chapters focusing specifically on you, your inner child, your hopes for the future, and your Sister-Self. Now we will shift the focus onto the people you desire to join you as you grow. In the next chapter, we will discuss how you can create authentic bonds with the people in your life who support your highest good.

**Repeat after me: Whether I know it or not,
I am always moving toward my deepest desires.**

10

Casting for Companionship

Be Different. Together.

> "Without a community of sense, an individual cannot keep hold of her radical insights, she becomes confused, she forgets what she knew."
>
> – Marilyn Frye, *Willful Virgin*

The Unruly Retreat is produced almost exclusively by women from top to bottom. From our photographers to our project managers to our guests, I spend time around a lot of women, and as such, the concept of feminine companionship is not one I teach at Unruly; it's a concept that Unruly has taught me. The community we keep around us is so important on this journey, and I have had the opportunity to work through how to be a better companion in my personal and professional life through my work with Unruly. While being authentically rebellious starts as a highly individual experience, your truest performance is only complete when you can do so in the company of others. This is not to say that we aren't enough on our own, but rather, this journey is best realized when we have a strong network of support we can lean on. And our network is strongest when we can function as a collective, working toward a common reality while also holding space for the ways in which we are all different and unique. The truth is, we cannot be Unruly alone. At least not forever. Your life is not a one-woman show. We all need a supporting cast, even if we are the main character.

In a group performance, the magic is in witnessing the spectacle of many different elements coming together seamlessly. Each performer changes the group's chemistry, so it is vital to have performers in roles that highlight their unique abilities. When the chemistry is right, the differences between individual performers make the entire production more compelling. Even solo performances require a team effort; you can't perform onstage while also handling lighting and sound cues. We need each other.

Finding women to support your growth authentically can be challenging. At some points, you might decide you're better off going at it alone. It can be tempting to fold into yourself and focus only on creating the life you want. (Guilty!) This may happen in seasons, and that's okay. But it's problematic in the long term for a few reasons: First, you will put undue stress and pressure on yourself to figure everything out on your own, which will inevitably lead to burnout and potential mental health issues like depression or anxiety. Humans are social creatures. We are not meant to live in isolation. This "I can do it all by myself" energy can be dangerous for you, and it is actually rooted in capitalistic, colonial worldviews. The basis of many ancestral cultures and traditional practices rely on community support. They recognized thousands of years ago that humans work best as a group. If you attempt an Unruly journey without outside support, it can *literally* be hazardous for your health. Some studies cite that almost 60 percent of Americans regularly feel lonely—a rate at which, according to cognitive scientist Laurie Santos, is higher than the rates of obesity in America.[1] Julianne Holt-Lunstad, PhD, a professor of psychology, says the "lack of social connection heightens health risks as much as smoking fifteen cigarettes a day or having alcohol use disorder."[2] Think about that for a second: a large number of people are living through an individual yet collective loneliness epidemic that could seriously harm our health.

Even with Western science aside, individual mindsets generally do not work in a spiritual or religious sense. Whether we congregate in churches or build covens, collectives, or other groups, Black folks in particular have always gathered together to spiritually develop ourselves, and therefore, our communities. Socially, Black folks have typically lived in tight-knit communities, whether the group members are blood-related or not. From aunties and uncles to play cousins and godparents, there is always someone to talk to or confide in, and there is always someone there to watch your back. Yet the individualistic nature of American society encourages us to be alone. We are rewarded for our individual pursuits, our manicured and fenced-in lawns, our educational achievements, and anything else that can point back to our individual merit. We have been deluded into thinking we can and should do it alone. Because we've lived in this individualistic society for so long, some of us have even learned to judge our self-worth by how much we can achieve alone. Spoiler alert: *You cannot build a new world alone.* I like to say: I might not change *the* world, but I can change *a* world. With the support of other Unruly women, we have the ability to create a world where everyone has the tools to live the life of their dreams.

> **An Unruly woman's self-preservation rests on her ability to find other women who share her core values and are active co-creators of a similar shared vision.**

"Okay, Shelah . . . but how do I find women to build with?" Well, let's start with what *not* to do. Take a front row seat to learn from my mistakes, so you don't have to repeat them.

When I was in my twenties, I thought it was silly to think deeply about intentionally creating friendships. In my mind, they just happened. You meet someone, share common interests, and boom . . . you're friends. But as I got older and my needs evolved and became more complex, I realized that I put more effort into planning an outfit than I did into curating my friendships, and because of this, I was often left with unsatisfying relationships. Without consciously knowing it, I had been making friends with a pyramid formation, as I call it, for most of my life. I would categorize my relationships like levels of a pyramid.

This is the way I imagined it:

> **Level 1:** The bottom tier is the largest portion of the pyramid, and as such it includes the most people. These would be our acquaintances, those we are friendly with but don't necessarily divulge personal information to.

Level 2: On the next, slightly smaller level, are our friends, those we are more selective about and have more personal relationships with.

Level 3: At the top is our smallest, most intimate tier. This is where our close friends and family live on the pyramid.

This pyramid-style view of friendship led me to make some big mistakes when it came to friendship. Let's break them down.

MISTAKE #1: I ASSUMED FAMILY AND/OR LONGTIME FRIENDS SHOULD AUTOMATICALLY BE IN MY TOP TIER.

This mistake came from a good place, in the sense that I want to be close to my family, I love them, and I value them, so I naturally thought they would be the perfect inner circle. In some cases, they can be, and if that's the case for you, excellent—but this is not to be *assumed*. Family systems are complex, sometimes volatile, and highly interdependent. If you are challenging the family system in any way or living a lifestyle that members can't easily relate to or approve of, then having them in your inner circle will only make your journey more challenging.

In the same way that shared DNA doesn't mean someone is willing or able to be the type of close friend you need, shared experiences don't either. Length of time does always correlate with a shared understanding or worldview. Especially if, over time, you are evolving and growing, while they aren't. Your inner circle should only house people who understand you deeply, support your growth, and share similar values.

MISTAKE #2: I THOUGHT RELATIONSHIPS ARE ONLY GOOD IF THEY LAST.

I've always heard good friends are hard to come by, so I was determined to keep the ones I had. I thought that no one could ever know or understand me like women who had known me since I was a child. I also didn't want my friends to think I'd outgrown them, so I kept them firmly in my inner circle—even though I didn't feel wholly seen or understood by them. I prioritized the length of the relationship above the quality of the relationship.

During my college and post-college years, I traveled abroad, teaching, acting, and expanding my view of myself and the world. I was not the same Shelah I was when my childhood friendships started. I wasn't the timid five-year-old looking to make new friends at school anymore. I didn't realize it then, but it can be hard to shift out of the dynamic that was present when the relationship first started. As my therapist said to me, "The energy a thing was created with stays with the thing." When I started my relationship with them, I sought acceptance and belonging as a child—making me an expert people-pleaser and at times, a dishonest version of myself. This was the foundation of our relationship, and that was the dynamic that they understood from me. I had extreme respect, love, and care for these women because we had gone through our most formative years together. They knew me in a way that nobody else understood—but that was also the problem: Even fifteen years after meeting them, I would spontaneously shift into performing five-year-old Shelah without even realizing it, comfortable in that dynamic that I'd grown into with them, even if it went against the growth I wanted for myself. The inability to shed this dynamic meant I couldn't move forward in my healing journey because the new Shelah didn't fit into the old dynamic—and they no longer understood the new Shelah, who was more self-assured and less willing to people-please to her own detriment.

I had to let go of the idea that a friendship is only good if it lasts forever. I reminded myself that we don't own people; we experience them. If you find yourself constantly being misunderstood, feeling unheard, or not having a genuine common ground to stand on with your friends, family or community, then it might be time to examine the life of that relationship. Because of this, those friends and I went through a period of disconnection, but we eventually rebuilt a friendship dynamic that was healthier and more appropriate for our current situation—for the people we'd grown to be, and wanted to grow to be, since first meeting in childhood.

When you inspect your relationships through this lens, you might find that it's time to part ways or it's just time for a shift in the dynamic that will be more accommodating to your personal growth. Either way, change is not to be feared. Shifts are a natural and healthy part of deep relationships. And if for some reason the relationship doesn't make it through that shift, then ask yourself, how deep was that bond to begin with?

MISTAKE #3: I PUT TOO MUCH PRESSURE ON MY CLOSE FRIENDS.

"If you feel any intense pain or cramping, you need to go the emergency room immediately because it could be an ectopic pregnancy," my ob-gyn warned me.

I was so optimistic this time. It had been almost a year since my last miscarriage, and I just knew I was going to *fix* myself, make it right this time. I had finally healed from the trauma of sharing my first miscarriage on national television and all the social commentary that came with that. I did all the things in order to heal. I went to a holistic doctor, changed my diet, switched up my workout routine, balanced my hormone levels, engaged in new breathwork practices, and re-committed to my meditation practice. I was determined to heal whatever stood before me and becoming a mother.

After almost a year of going the holistic route with diet changes, an exercise regimen, yoni steams, herbal teas, supplements, spiritual cleansings, fertility meditations, Reiki, and acupuncture without getting pregnant, I finally broke down and decided to see a fertility specialist. I dragged myself into the office, as everything in my body told me I shouldn't have to be doing this. I should just get pregnant without having to try. As I stepped into the office, I mourned the carefree nature that I would lay to rest with this appointment. I had to grieve that I would not just happen to get pregnant, I would have to arrange it. I did not want to need this type of help getting pregnant. I had internalized this idea that I could have a successful pregnancy if I simply connected more with my divine feminine energy—and so having to see a specialist meant that I wasn't doing it right enough. Or that's what I told myself, at least. During this year, I had slowly started to change, regressing into previous patterns of depression and anxiety. I trusted people less. Trusted my body less. Trusted myself even less. And, I will be honest, I was not the best person during this time. My quest for motherhood made me selfish, self-absorbed, and callous. These were symptoms of my deep pain, disappointment, and isolation.

Yet during my very first bloodwork appointment at the fertility clinic, they discovered I was already six weeks pregnant! *I did it*, I thought. My hard work had paid off. I had healed myself.

But there was a minor issue: they couldn't see any evidence of an embryo in my uterus. At the time, the doctor attributed this to how early the pregnancy was. I was living in two worlds simultaneously, one of infinite possibility and hope, and another where I reminded myself to be logical and not to get too excited yet.

A few days later, the pain started at around 8 pm. It felt like the worst period cramps I had ever experienced. I couldn't eat or do much of anything. I tried to sleep but was jolted out of bed at midnight by the pain. I didn't know what to do. I hadn't told anyone outside my close friends that I was pregnant and my husband was out of town on a work trip. I tried to meditate, but the anxiety was swelling in my chest, making breathing increasingly harder. I grabbed my phone and texted my close friend group chat: 911 EMERGENCY IS ANYONE UP?

I waited a few minutes. No response.

I called them one by one. No answer.

I initiated a group FaceTime. Again no answer.

In a panic, I dressed and drove to the emergency room myself. They couldn't find anything wrong with me, so they sent me home and told me to call my ob-gyn in the morning. I was relieved to hear my HCG levels were normal, despite them not being able to locate the source of my pain. At least my baby was okay.

I drove home and just hoped the pain would subside. Thankfully, I drifted off to sleep—but not for long. Around 2 am, I was awakened again by the same excruciating pain. I swallowed my pride and called my sister, who worked in the ER and drove back to the hospital. I called my friend group on FaceTime again, but still no answer.

The doctor entered the room and said my worst fear in one short sentence, "Your HCG levels have dropped in half."

I was losing my baby.

To say that I was crushed is an understatement. I felt like someone had switched my world from color to black and white. I attribute that moment to a fundamental change in my brain chemistry. I was not the same after that moment. Having another miscarriage after all the hard work I'd put into "fixing" myself reaffirmed what I already feared to be true about myself: I am not worthy.

For a while, these resurfacing beliefs won. The whispers in the dark amplified until they were all I could hear. In a distorted attempt to work through my grief, I removed myself from our group chat and stopped communicating with my close friends group. I had decided that I was better off alone. My rationale was that when I needed them the most, they hadn't answered my call, so I didn't want to burden them with my constant low mood and sadness anymore.

Looking back on that night, I honor the totality and validity of my emotional experience. I honor my ability to feel deeply, to access hope, and also the courage to feel pain. But, in retrospect, I handled those feelings very poorly. My friends have whole lives, jobs, and families; why should I expect them to answer a call in the middle of the night? They had already held my hand unwaveringly through years of ups and downs.

Why would I let this one moment serve as evidence that they weren't there for me? To be fair, there were signs that our dynamic needed shifting before this, but still, in this moment, the truth was I felt rejected by my own future child, and I was projecting that pain onto them. I was putting too much pressure on a few people to meet all of my emotional needs. This season of my life was getting increasingly complex and demanding, and to expect that group of women to keep up with the changes in my life when they had ongoing stresses and pressures in their own lives was where I went wrong. I needed more diversity in my support system in order to meet the growing needs of my life. One small group could not be my everything, my full and total support system.

For a long time, I failed to diversify my friendship groups because I "already had friends." I wouldn't let in new people because I didn't think I needed or wanted more friends. My idea was, well, I have this group of deeply connected friends; we talk about everything, and I get everything I need from them, so why look elsewhere? But without knowing it, I was overwhelming them. I was operating off of this idea that if a friendship is close, it must be *super deep*. And if a friend is close, I have to be able to tell them *everything* and talk to them about *everything*. I felt that I wasn't being authentic or honest if I couldn't talk about every aspect of my life with my closest friends. This is the problem I discovered with the pyramid model. By design, it puts a heavy amount of pressure on your inner circle because they are the only people that feel very close to you.

Instead, following the companionship model means having a more nuanced standard of friendship that supports your whole evolution while also showing care and concern for the labor and output of the people you love. As I write this book, I have a diverse and healthy friendship life where I allow connections to flourish based on shared interests and a shared vision. Rather than arbitrarily placing people close to me based on how long we've known each other, I now use my own discernment to navigate each individual relationship. I identify the strengths and skills of each friend and engage with them in ways that allow us both to show up as our best selves. Now my inner circle consists of all different kinds of people: I have friends that have also done reality TV, friends who are deep in their spiritual practice, and women who are also on their path to motherhood in my closest circle. And I did it by following my method for companionship, which we'll dive into next.

Unruly Inquiry

Imagine you have a magic wand that can create a companionship dynamic that perfectly reflects your needs and desires. What kinds of people and qualities come to mind? For the rest of this chapter and afterward, allow this vision of yourself to be your life vest. If at any point, you find yourself resisting this process, return to this image of your desired companion.

CAST YOUR COMPANIONS

I am using the word "companion" here instead of friends. I don't think you need help making friends necessarily. Friends are people who you enjoy spending time with or have shared interests and/or experiences with. Friends happen through work; via online spaces or groups; workout classes; school; or through shared connections. Friends are important, but from what I have learned, friends happen, whereas *companions are curated*. Companions are the friends that travel with you over time on your journey. Companions are actively growing and evolving alongside you and with you. And because of this, companions take a little more intentionality than friends do. Women have been conditioned to give specific, intentional, and continued energy into crafting lives with men, and sometimes only have their leftover energy for friendship. This is not a judgment; it's an opportunity for us to think more deeply about how we can use the same type of deliberate energy to be in community with our sisters. In the rest of this chapter, I will share my top findings that I've learned along the way to support you in casting Unruly Companions who will enrich your life and grow with you.

Learning from my past mistakes, use these revelations to curate your cast of Companions moving forward. This section will help you attract Companions who will be most supportive of your Unruly journey.

Identify Your Values
Liking the same movies or foods is good enough for friends or acquaintances, but for Unruly Companions, those who will travel with you on your self-discovery journey, you must also align on your core values. Your core values are the ethics and traits you use to guide your daily decisions, like integrity, compassion, and respect. They are the ideals you feel very strongly about and would defend ferociously. When you are in alignment with your core values, you feel proud, settled, and in alignment. When you go against them, you feel discomfort, nervousness, and shame. An Unruly Companion has the ability to engage deeply and intimately with your core values. This doesn't mean she always will—not every interaction requires depth and intimacy—but she *can*. You are a part of the modern cohort of conscious-minded, educated, social-media-savvy, well-traveled, therapy-going women who want to go beyond social ritual and politeness. You can only know others as deeply as you know yourself. The first step in attracting Companions is by being one to yourself. Remember, you attract what you are. We can only be good partners with people if we are honest in communication with ourselves.

Take this time to get clear on what matters to you most, what you seek in life, and what you stand for. If you already know your values clearly, then this will be easy for you. If not, take this time to gain more clarity or insight. It might also be a good moment to see if your values need any updating.

To begin, identify **three to five** of your core values. These are the values that matter to you the most, propel you into action, and inspire you to keep creating, even when it's challenging. For example, my core values are spiritual growth, genuine connection, and pleasure.

If you have trouble identifying your core values, I can guarantee you that you also have some degree of challenge in developing friendships that feel good to you. As I said, we attract what we are, and if you don't know what you are, what you attract will likely be haphazard and less than you ultimately desire. If you're feeling stuck on what your values are, go over what you spent your time, energy, and money on in the last month. This can serve as a starting point. Reviewing where you put your resources shows what matters to you the most. Obviously, your core value is not UberEats, but if you review your last month and you notice that you spent a lot of time in nature, or you do an exercise class weekly, this could mean that health and wellness are very important to you. If you look back and notice you spent a lot of time engaging with social justice content and community endeavors this past month, then you may value justice and community-building very deeply. If you spent a lot of time with family, then maybe family is a core value for you.

It's important to note that your core values do not need to be exactly the same as your friends, but you want to make sure that they are at least *complementary*. For example, if one of your core values is spirituality, it will be hard to build on an intimate level with someone who doesn't value that at all. This doesn't mean they don't have a place in your life, this just means they would not be appropriate as an intimate Companion.

Again, knowing your values helps you place people appropriately in your life. The most essential truth that I want you to take away from this part of the book is that while someone in your life doesn't have to actively support every value you hold dear, they absolutely shouldn't *undermine* any core values. They don't have to support everything you do, but they can't actively go against any of your most important values.

After you gain clarity on your values, you can use them as a guide for connection with current and future Companions. If you feel comfortable, you can also share them in conversation and ask your Companion to share hers. This will give you both more information about each other, and ultimately allow you to become better Companions to each other.

Examples of Core Values:

Kindness	Joy
Justice	Honesty
Equity	Fun
Respect	Family
Pleasure	Health
Abundance	Spirituality

Your Emotional Algorithm for Companionship

When we talked about manifesting, we created an Emotional Algorithm, and we will apply the same concept here. In this case, the Emotional Algorithm you're building is the *primary* emotional experience you'd like to have with your Unruly Companions. Use the Serious Daydreaming meditation below to help you identify the main emotional experience you want to have with your Companions.

Meditation Moment

Find yourself in a comfortable position. When you feel ready, close your eyes and use any breathing technique to center yourself. When you feel completely calm and centered, find yourself in front of a door. On the other side of the door, you will enter the life of your Sister-Self, who has curated a healthy network of Unruly Companions. When you are ready, open the door and meet your Sister-Self. While you are in her life, pay attention to any emotions you experience. When you feel complete, exit the door and return to the present moment.

What were the three main emotions you felt during the meditation? If you can't identify them or didn't experience any, write three that you would like to experience.

This is your Emotional Algorithm. You can revisit the activities I laid out in chapter 8 to strengthen your relationship with your Emotional Algorithm. Your EA is your guide for you to know when you are in alignment.

Be Honest about Your Expectations

All relationships are transactional to some degree, and this is not a negative thing to acknowledge; it's honest. Mismanaged expectations are one of the top reasons that friendships between women fall apart or are not mutually beneficial.

You can't honestly decide if someone is suitable for a particular role in your cast if you don't know what their role is in your story. Imagine the director of the 90s TV series *Martin* not specifying to the actors that the show is a comedy. Imagine the director auditioning only serious actors for the roles. The failure to communicate that expectation would have compromised the entire series.

Being honest about your expectations is fundamental for a healthy partnership or relationship with anyone, yet we often take this step for granted. We often expect people to just know what we expect from them and what we need. "She's my best friend; she should know I like flowers on my birthday." But why should she know this if you've never explicitly shared this with her? Shared space or shared experience does not always mean a shared understanding. It's your job, Main Character, to lay down clear, honest expectations about your companion exchange.

This might be your first time thinking through companionship in this way, so, as we continue on in getting a deeper understanding of why some relationships in our lives may not serve our overall progress in life, let's honor three important truths right now before moving forward.

Truth 1: You will not get this 100 percent right the first time—and what about it?

Truth 2: No one person will ever meet all your expectations—and what about it?

Truth 3: You will sometimes fall short of your expectations—and what about it?

Say it with me: *And what about it?* Acknowledge your humanness and honor your courage for attempting to create a new dynamic between yourself and your future or current companions. Instead of trying to tiptoe around these truths, gently hold them close to you and notice that they did not bite you. These truths are expected as part of the process. It's not a matter of *if* they will show up, but a matter of *when*. And when they do, do not internalize them as a personal defect but rather a natural part of the process of deepening your understanding of your own needs and values, and how those around you do or don't serve that for you.

Write a short sentence describing what you expect from a fulfilling Companion relationship. Keep the expectations to three to four sentences. Reference any details that came to you in your meditation.

Example: I expect encouragement and alignment along our spiritual growth journey. I expect us to connect and communicate in an authentic way. I expect us to have grace with each other.

Of course, any relationship in our lives requires reciprocity, so next, write what you are willing to exchange for someone meeting those expectations.

Example: In exchange, I will offer support and resources for their spiritual evolution. I will communicate honestly, take accountability for my actions, and speak up when something needs to be adjusted. I will provide opportunities for us both to experience joy.

You have now laid the foundation for what you and your Companion can expect on both ends. While I don't think you need to go so far as to interview potential candidates in a formal way, I do think having your expectations and exchange clarified for you will promote healthy connection with others. If someone hears your expectation and exchange descriptions, they will know immediately if they are a Companion or not. So, if you're trying to introduce this idea to someone and their face automatically turns sour, that is all you need to know! They are not the person to support these values. The more honest you are at this step, both with yourself and with them, the easier finding and keeping Companions will be.

Direct Your Cast

Now, this is arguably the most valuable lesson in this chapter: proximity. How much access does a person have to you? In order to cast the people in your life in their appropriate roles, you need to consider how close they are currently in your life and how close you want them to be. Do you want this person to be closer to you, or do you want them to actually have less proximity to you as you move forward with your Unruly growth journey?

Remember the pyramid friendship model I referenced at the start of the chapter? The pyramid model is too rigid to truly encompass the complexity of human connection. Life changes, people change, we change. You need a model for your Companions that can adapt just as you do. You need to direct your cast. A cast is fluid, flexible, and ever-changing. A cast is always in motion, but there is still harmony. There are levels of closeness in a cast, but it's not rigid in the way a pyramid structure has to be.

Imagine you are in the center of a circle and your support network orbits around you. With that image in mind, how close would you like someone to be to you? What level of closeness does each woman have with you? Does she know the intimate details of your personal life? Do you only see her once in a while for a lunch date? Do you only see her once a year for a girls' trip? There's much more variety than just "close" or "far" to choose from. Recognizing the various levels of proximity that you're looking for is valuable and necessary.

For your cast, I want you to conceptualize three levels of proximity to work with: Leads, Series Regulars, and Cameos. While this may seem similar to the pyramid model with its three levels, in a cast, people are organized much more intentionally based on core values and expectations, as opposed to being automatically placed in any category. They are cast—by you. And the cast can always be updated. This is an organic process that will take time. As we progress, know that you don't have to cast all three levels. Work with what you have and build as you go. If you only have one trusted companion right now, that's a great place to start.

To begin, create a list of your potential companion pool in your journal that could fit in at least one of the three proximity levels. One note: there will be friends or family who are important to you but aren't necessarily Unruly Companions; they would be considered a "background actor." Background actors are integral for creating a world on screen and making a scene come to life, but they are not necessary for moving the narrative forward. In your life, they are essential for a healthy social life and are worthy of mutual respect and care. However, for the purposes of this exercise, let's focus on women who can engage in deep companionship and truly support your core values.

Now that you have your potential Companion pool, you can officially begin casting.

Leads: In television, lead actors have the most time on screen and are integral to moving the story forward. They likely appear in almost every scene, and the audience often develops a close relationship with them. For example, the lead in the sitcom

Martin is Martin Lawrence (Martin), and in *The Fresh Prince of Bel-Air*, it's Will Smith (Will). Similarly, in your life, leads have the closest proximity to you and, therefore, the most access to you.

Leads have the capacity and willingness to nurture you living in your truth. Refer back to your notes. Who would be a Lead in your cast? This person would have the most access to you, and be very important to your life moving forward. If you have none of these at the moment, that is okay, too. I am actually in between Leads right now, so I am using this time to nurture myself just a little more until I find a new Lead. If you don't have a Lead, think of this exercise as an invitation for the right woman to show up in your life to fill that role.

Series Regulars: In a TV show, Series Regulars are not necessarily in every episode, but they are still a part of the primary cast. They are recurring actors that contribute to the season's progression but are not individually integral to the main story. In *The Fresh Prince of Bel-Air,* Will's best friend Jazzy Jeff wasn't in every episode, but when he did appear on screen, the audience knew to expect some laughs and for him to get thrown out of the front door by Uncle Phil. Similarly, your series regulars are those who you might not have consistent contact with, but they contribute meaningfully to your growth over time.

For example, I have a friend who I don't speak to every day, but we both share an interest in financial wellness. She will occasionally send me workshops and books to learn from, and I'll do the same. Even though we don't speak daily, we directly contribute to each other's growth. Take a moment to identify your Series Regulars in your journal.

Cameos: Finally, Cameos give the audience a sense of novelty and can allow the storyline to go in an unexpected direction with a brand-new character. This is often when fictional and real worlds collide, like when hip-hop legend Biggie Smalls was suddenly in the middle of Martin's apartment. He would deliver a simple one-liner like, "What's up, guys?" and the audience would go wild. While exciting, Cameos don't *have* to stick around in order to add value. It's very much understood that you probably won't see the person again for the rest of the season, and that's perfectly fine.

Think of your Cameos as people you don't need ongoing interaction or support from, but you both add value to each other when you do interact. They're kind of like that cousin you only see once a year, but when you do, you have the most fulfilling time together.

As you grow and evolve, new versions of yourself will emerge and you may have different needs and boundaries as a result. Because of this, I recommend you revisit this process at least once a year or when you go through significant shifts in your life.

Meditation Moment

Choose a name on your list that you are having trouble placing. Imagine yourself sitting across from this person on your list. How does it feel to be near them? Do you want them a little closer to you? Do you want them a bit farther from you? Should she be a Lead? A Series Regular? A Cameo? Find what level of proximity feels the best in your body and trust that this is the right one. Remember, you don't have to share this information with them or treat them differently because of it. This is purely for your benefit.

Quality over Quantity

A stage full of poorly casted actors is never as fulfilling as a small ensemble that is perfectly cast. Don't put pressure on yourself to have a large cast right away. This chapter is about community, but it's primarily about you becoming a better friend to yourself *first*. Getting clear on your values, being honest about your expectations, and managing the proximity of your cast demonstrates a deep care you have for yourself and to those around you. Build your cast in a way that feels good to you, and don't worry about how many people you have. You don't need all the people, just the best people—for you.

Nurture Your Cast

When you do have your cast, your job is to nurture them. Healthy relationships are reciprocal, so this section will give you some things to remember as you continue to pour into the people you care about. Have fun with these suggestions and keep in mind that the goal is for you to pour into people who are also pouring into you, but that doesn't have to be laborious. A little can go a long way.

Be Intentional: Being intentional will allow you to focus on quality over quantity, so you don't feel overwhelmed. Plan dates, meetups, or other moments of connection with your cast. Use this as an opportunity to have the experiences you desire instead of expecting them to just happen. Is it important for you to be celebrated on your birthday? Then plan the birthday vibe you want and communicate with your squad. If there's any role in particular you want them to have, communicate it openly without expectation and let them decide what they have the capacity to do. Scheduling and note-taking will go a long way here. Make a note of their birthdays, anniversaries, or special days they celebrate. As for me,

I put everything—*everything*—in my calendar. If it's not in my calendar, did it ever really exist to begin with? You can also take note of any big achievements they have coming up and find a way to celebrate them. Send a text, mail a card, send flowers, share on socials, or even plan a dinner or a get-together. Being intentional creates the circumstances for you to have meaningful connection instead of just hoping for them to happen spontaneously.

Release the Pressure: In the previous section I asked you to make space for intention or specific action toward what you want. Now I am encouraging you to release expectations around this process. Many things can be true at the same time. There will be moments that are super-curated and planned, but don't make that the standard for connection. Especially in a social media age, where events are produced just to be captured for a digital audience, there is a risk of trading genuine connection for aesthetics. Make space for serendipity, flexibility, and the mundane. Not every link-up has to be Instagram-worthy. Invite your girls over for a no-pressure hangout where you all just talk, order takeout, and catch up. Go to a park without the pressure of a stylized picnic, you get my drift? Move forward with ease, and when you can, release expectations from yourself and others. This freedom will allow for genuine connections to bloom.

Work Together: This tip is a game changer for busy women who already have so much on their plates. There's always work to be done, right? So why not do it together? Offer to help your Companion clean her house. Bring wine, put on music you both enjoy, and split up the work that needs to be done. If you feel inspired, help her load the dishwasher or fold a load of laundry. Do you both work from home? Work together. Enjoy eating lunch together and maybe indulge in a celebratory end-of-workday Netflix session. If one or both of you have children, attend an activity already on the calendar (like dance class or a Little League game) and just spend time. You can also arrange a Target or grocery-shopping date where you all simply get groceries together. Frame these moments as an opportunity to lighten the load for one or both of you. In this way, you don't have to pause your life to be friends; instead, you can integrate them into your life.

Surprise and Delight: Have you ever signed up for a mailing list, entered your birthday and completely forgot about it, only to be surprised with a free gift on your birthday? This is surprise and delight, a marketing concept where companies are encouraged to surprise their customers with unexpected gifts or special recognition. I think that this strategy can also work magic in friendships. You can schedule this in your calendar like I do, just to hold myself accountable, or you can let your spirit guide you. Think of ways you can surprise your cast with a small gesture to let them know you're thinking of them. See a cute trinket at the store that reminds you of her? Pop it in the mail or give it to her the next time you meet. Saw something online that made you think of someone? Screenshot and text it over. Passing a bakery that you know your friend loves? Grab something for her, get a gift card, or simply send a photo to let her know she's on your mind. Again, a little goes a long way. The goal is to make meaningful touch points with your cast.

THE END OF THE ROAD: FRIENDSHIP BREAKUPS

There are copious amounts of movies, books, and resources guiding women through romantic breakups, but very few resources to navigate the devastation of a friendship breakup. As Joy Harden Bradford relates in her book *Sisterhood Heals*, "Only we intimately know the interiors of another's worlds.

Sadly, this is also why betrayals and disappointments by our sisters cut the deepest and why the loss of sisterfriendship feels so devastating."[3] As you complete these exercises, you may realize that you've grown apart from certain friends and it's time to cut the cord, or you may be thinking about a time when you experienced your own friendship breakup that you haven't quite mourned. If that's the case, use the tips in this section to guide yourself through a friendship breakup because, unfortunately, they are a natural part of being a friend. It's not a matter of if but when.

Give Yourself Space to Grieve

Just grieve. Mourn. Cry. Let it out. In many ways, you are laying to rest the dream you all had as friends, which deserves a proper send-off. Attempting to bypass the mourning stage will simply cause you to repress your pain, only for it to inevitably express itself in some other way. If you don't get these difficult emotions out now, you will roll them over into other friendship dynamics. Use everything you've learned this far in your Unruly journey to make peace with all the emotions that come up during this time.

Grieving Options:

> If you have access, talk to a therapist.

> Do a Serious Daydreaming session and ask your Sister-Self what she would do.

> Do a Serious Daydreaming session and visualize yourself one year from now, completely healed from your present pain.

Write a goodbye letter to your friend to get your feelings out. But do not send it! Your grieving is *your* process; it is *your* time to get everything out without a filter. Sending a letter from this place could be very hurtful to someone else. Sending the letter also re-centers the other person in your grieving process. Only you can give yourself closure. Only you can make peace with your reality. Reject the urge to shift this burden onto someone else.

Engage your creative side. Write, draw, paint, sew, etc. Find a creative outlet to channel your feelings.

Write a eulogy to the friendship and read it out loud.

Take Inventory
After you've spent time processing your feelings, now it's time to step back from your emotions and engage with your nonjudgmental, curious side. Emphasis on nonjudgmental.

- In what ways did you contribute to the end of this friendship?

- In what ways did they contribute to the end of the friendship?

- If you could go back in time, would you do anything differently?

- Are there any lessons you learned that can be applied to current or future relationships?

- Are there any red flags that you ignored earlier? If you answered yes, how can you use this information to trust yourself more next time?

Don't Take It Personal

Shout-out to Don Miguel Ruiz's *The Four Agreements* for this tip. It's not easy, but when you grasp this concept, it is so freeing. If you feel you've reached the end of a friendship, it can be an utterly devastating blow. I know in my case, it felt worse than a romantic breakup. Was it all fake? Did we ever have a real connection? How could we end our relationship after all the time we shared? Approaching the end of a relationship with someone you've been so vulnerable with can make you question everything. This is normal, but try not to internalize the surge of emotions and make stories out of them. When you take something personally, you center yourself in a story you've created in your mind. *How could she do that to me? How could she treat me that way?*

Consider that, on a certain level, someone else's actions have absolutely nothing to do with you. After going through a heartbreaking end with a dear friend, I realized that her distance wasn't because she didn't care, it was because she was overwhelmed with life and burnt out. I understand this is not easy at all, but if you take this personally, you cut off the pathway to healing. This might be the end forever, or just for right now, but as much as you can, don't take it personally.

As we close this chapter, take a moment to honor yourself for coming this far in your Unruly journey. No matter what stage of the journey you are in, it's important to acknowledge yourself adequately and take inventory of the hard work you've put in thus far. On the flip side, sometimes it's just as important to do absolutely nothing at all. In the next chapter, I will introduce the concept of rest and help explain why it is a nonnegotiable when it comes to sustained evolution and growth.

Repeat after me: I am supported, loved, and cared for.

Unfixed

11

A Dramatic Pause

Please Sit Your Ass Down Somewhere

I was lucky enough to see *Hamilton* at The Public Theater before it went to Broadway. The Public is an off-Broadway theater, so it has a more intimate setting than many Broadway theaters. I was up close and personal with the actors. I was especially enthralled by Phillipa Soo, who played Eliza Hamilton. During her performance of the song "Burn," her use of tempo moved me to the core. In the song, she expressed the heartache she felt from being betrayed by her husband. There's a moment where she pauses right before burning the letters he wrote her. In that five-second pause, I felt a static connection with not only the character Eliza but also the actual feeling of betrayal. I was not only relating; I was being realized. That moment was no longer hers; it was ours.

There is power in a pause. In theater, and in life.

I've noticed that novice actors are generally too afraid to pause. The actor fears stopping because that might give the audience a moment to create an opinion about the performance or decide they're not interested. The novice interprets a quick tempo as intensity, when the opposite can also be true. A purposeful pause creates the space for developing a relationship between the performer and the audience.

Rest as a concept is similar to the dramatic pause in the theater. Rest allows you to develop a relationship with your inner guidance. As you move forward in your Unruly journey, your lifeline will be your ability to stop, to pause. Your ability to not do anything, ironically, will help you achieve everything. Have you ever seen an overtired child fight sleep? It's maddening to watch them run around in a hazy state of exhaustion, knowing they just need rest. My family's response to that behavior would be a loving-yet-stern "Please sit your ass down somewhere!" This chapter is your reminder to sit your ass down sometimes—respectfully. This is your reminder to rest. Rest makes space for communion. It is at the core of self-realization.

During the 2020 lockdown, I, along with the rest of the world, was forced to think more deeply about rest. During this time, I came across the Nap Ministry, founded by the Nap Bishop and founder of the Nap Ministry, Tricia Hersey. I was mesmerized by radical rest and the idea of rest as a tool for decolonization and resistance. I am genuinely in awe of Hersey's dedication to interrupting brutal systems via sleep, dreaming, and rest. She reminded me of what I already knew deep down but was ignoring: the importance of rest for the Unruly woman. This chapter is inspired by my own personal journey with rest, what I've learned, and tips for you to incorporate more rest into your life.

YOU DO NOT HAVE TO EARN REST

This one took me a while to digest, as I had always conceptualized rest as something to be earned. I cleaned my room, so now I can watch TV. I did my homework, so now I can veg out on the couch. The problem with this is it marries the idea of labor and rest. It tells you that without labor, there is no rest. It implies that only after you have worked hard enough, then can you rest. But under late-stage capitalism, where we have evolved from exchanging commodities to *being* commodities, rest is essential to maintain your humanity. Often, you do the work, but the rest never comes. And if you do not rest, you cannot connect with your inner guidance and wisdom.

Popular advice tells you to push yourself beyond your limits for the sake of being successful. And women pay the highest price for this type of rhetoric due to the invisible domestic labor that's also demanded of us. I have seen friends go from being women with diverse, dynamic lives to full-time fire-putter-outers who barely have a moment to think quietly, let alone claim any semblance of meaningful rest.

I have privilege, agency, and freedom that many women don't, so I feel responsible for speaking up on this topic so my sisters can all access the rest they deserve. Women have been socialized to anchor their own sense of self in caretaking and giving to others. We have been taught to be more comfortable following than leading, we have been told we are better seen than heard, and we have been convinced that the world is entitled to our free mental, emotional, and physical labor.

This idea is codified by the term "kinkeeping," created by sociologist Carolyn J. Rosenthal. Kinkeeping refers to the invisible labor subconsciously assigned to women because of their gender, that seeks to maintain or strengthen familial bonds.[1] I saw a brilliant analogy of this concept explained in a TikTok from a gender studies student. She said gender expectations on women are similar to going to the theater. The audience cheers for the actors at the show's end because that is the only labor they see and recognize. The audience does not clap for the lighting director, the stagehands, the ushers, or the dozens of other jobs necessary for the successful production they just witnessed.[2]

In this analogy, men are the actors, and women occupy the invisible positions. In our everyday lives, we remember important dates, order flowers, book birthday party venues, and purchase gifts for the children labeled "from Dad." Women are unconsciously expected to produce tremendous physical and emotional labor while seldom getting appropriate recognition. Being able to name something is the first step toward shifting it, so it's essential to name the invisible work expected of women so we can honor it and move toward a more equitable distribution of labor. An effective antidote to this unequal dynamic is rest. Opt out. Leave the dishes in the sink, don't send the card during your lunch break, and resist the urge to do one more thing before you sit down. Your worthiness is not connected to how much you can do. You are not a machine, and you are not the sum of your labor. This is true both in daily life and in your personal growth journey.

YOU DON'T HAVE TO EARN IT, BUT YOU DO HAVE TO TAKE IT

Most Western societies do not have an adequate framework for the rest we need. America is no exception. Until larger systems are put in place to protect women and our labor, we have to do the best we can with what we have. Chances are, you might be thinking, *I know I need to rest, but I can't.* I want to validate that thought because there is no real framework or support for women, especially Black women, to rest. But the point remains—you need rest in order to self-actualize, and no one is going to give you the space to rest. You must take it in whatever way you can. Know up front that you may stand out for doing this; you may even be criticized or framed as lazy. And what about it?

Be less focused on others' perceptions of you and more on the version of yourself that you are nurturing. The version of yourself that deserves to thrive. The more connected you become with your personal needs, the easier it will be to know when you need rest. A great place to start is by acknowledging the need to rest when you experience friction. Those moments where you just can't figure out the answer to a question, the idea isn't coming to you, or you're having trouble writing what should be a simple email, give yourself permission to stop. When you reach a pain point, honor it by resting instead of bulldozing.

Sometimes, the pain point is a sign that you need to course-correct altogether; other times, maybe a slight modification to the plan is required. Rest is the buttress for your humanity and your highest self.

I want you to match the rest to the energy output. You are refilling your cup. For example, if you're frustrated because you've been toiling away and haven't gotten the amount of work done in a day that you wanted, that may require an hour's nap, some leisure reading, or taking yourself to get your favorite ice cream. But let's say you spent months on a project at work—this will require a more significant amount of rest. You may need a twenty-four-hour solo staycation, a sick day, or a weekend of putting your phone on Do Not Disturb. You will find what works for your life. Your guide is to match the rest to the problem and allow your physical and mental body to experience meaningful rest.

It's not easy for women to rest; it can even seem impossible initially, so don't make this another thing on your to-do list. Release the pressure to get it *right*. You are creating a brand-new Unruly life, so give yourself grace as you do. Here are some options for how to get some much-needed rest.

SHORT REST OPTIONS

- Take yourself on a dinner or lunch date. Prepare for the date as if you were going to meet someone special. Choose a place that excites you. While on the date, challenge yourself to be present without a phone or other distractions. Think of this time as a space to recharge and reconnect with your star player.

- Go on a grounding nature walk barefoot without your cell phone.

- Take a luxurious bath or shower. Use your favorite oils, bath salts, candles, and a glass of wine if that suits you.

- One of my favorites is a self-pleasure break. Orgasms are excellent for releasing stress and tension.

- Get in a good laugh. Spend a few minutes watching something that gives you a genuine belly laugh.

- Sit in silence. Whether you meditate or just sit with yourself, put a timer on for five to ten minutes and be silent. Set the intention that the silence will energize you. You can also sit in your car for a few minutes if you need to get out of the house. You can sit in silence, or you can play your favorite music.

- Do something aimless that you enjoy, with no objective in mind.

DEEP REST OPTIONS

- Choose a destination within two hours of your home. Book a hotel or Airbnb with no other plans but to rest and experience pleasure. Refrain from going into a hyper-planning mode; that would defeat the purpose. Ask your higher self to guide you. Your goal is to rest. Even twenty-four hours can provide a world of difference.

- Take a solo trip somewhere you've always wanted to but couldn't find people to go with you. This could be an afternoon, a weekend, or longer.

- Take your inner child on the trip of her dreams. To do this, I recommend going by yourself or with friends, and not with children. The goal is for you to be the focus of the activity and to have rest.

- Put your phone on Do Not Disturb mode as soon as you wake up and leave it on all day. Extend it for a weekend if you'd like. To ease any worry, you can inform friends and family beforehand and create an emergency plan. For example, the iPhone has a setting where if someone calls you three times in a row, your phone will ring even though it's technically on Do Not Disturb. Be sure to silence all social media.

- At the beginning of the year, choose a designated rest time for yourself where no work will be done. This may take a little effort and preplanning, but the juice is worth the squeeze. Hersey, the founder of The Nap Ministry, does "No Work November" annually. I like to do it a week or so before Christmas, as it's my absolute favorite time of the year. Again, give yourself permission to find what works for you.

- See if you can schedule some rest in advance. Can you find an hour? Thirty minutes? A day? Plan your rest in the same way you plan everything else.

DREAM WORK

In the same way I believe in the power of Serious Daydreaming, I also believe in the power of dreaming. Both engage a version of play and fun that is often not considered part of one's healing tool kit. It can be so freeing to go beyond logical thought processes and step into the unknown, the magical, and the mystical.

There's a myth that a thing is only useful if it's productive, so it's no wonder many people have never even heard of dream work, let alone are open to it. Dreams are primarily framed as these odd, nonsensical, and sometimes vaguely meaningful content mashups that occur in your mind while you sleep. We are told that problem-solving or calling things forward requires active focus and intention. This can be true, but not always. I advocate for dream work as a respite from this labored thinking. After all, it is not guaranteed that even our best intentions, whether focused or productive, will be fruitful.

In the 2010 Invisible Gorilla Experiment conducted at Harvard University, viewers were asked to watch a short video of people passing a ball back and forth to each other. Scientists advised them to keep track of the number of passes. During the video, someone in a gorilla suit steps *directly into the middle of the frame*, beats their chest, and exits. At the end of the experiment, viewers were asked if they saw the gorilla. As the website for the experiment notes, "half of the people who watched the video and counted the passes missed the gorilla."[3] This psychological phenomenon is called selective attention, or the idea that when engaged in a task, we narrow our focus and ignore much of the sensory data around us. What are we missing that's right in front of our eyes?

If you choose, dream time can be an opportunity to see things you may not be able to see in your waking life. What if you could solve problems while you sleep? What if you could heal yourself while you sleep?

The ego will tell us that we must always be in the driver's seat in our healing, but I disagree. I would argue that some of your most profound healing can happen without you even knowing it or realizing it is happening in the moment. Sleep is one of the most basic and productive ways to both rest and heal your mind, body, and spirit. In addition to giving our minds and bodies a much-needed reset, sleep can also be a time of creation.

The following dream-play idea is a fun way to engage with your subconscious and give yourself a chance to make rest productive. Rest does not need to be productive, but it can be. Rest is productive enough in that it energizes you, heals you, and regenerates you, but there's also a lot of opportunity to play while you rest. Below is a quick breakdown of an activity you can try to experiment with dream play.

Dream Play: Sleep On It

This activity is a tool you can use to develop a playful relationship with rest and your subconscious, with an added productivity bonus if that's your thing.

First, identify what you'd like to happen while you sleep. Maybe you need guidance, an answer to a question, or you simply want to feel something you're not feeling in your waking life. Ask for this experience to happen while you sleep. Write down your dream desire in your journal or on a piece of paper next to your bed. Examples of dream-play topics include:

> If you have to write a difficult email but can't find the words to do it, ask that it be written for you and then attempt to write it first thing the following morning.

> Request to have a specific dream in a fun and whimsical location.

> Request a dream that brings you compassion and gentleness.

Call on your subconscious to continue working while you rest. If it helps, you can visualize your subconscious as a little work center in your brain, happily toiling away while you dream. To make this practice even more effective, you can play positive affirmations while you sleep, a healing sound-bath track, or binaural beats.

Set an intention to receive a response to a question. Request that you be given a kind, straightforward answer that you can understand and recall. If you're requesting an emotional experience, like feeling loved or comforted, state that request clearly in the minutes before going to sleep. Express gratitude in advance for receiving the guidance you need.

In the morning, write down anything you remember from your sleep, even if it doesn't seem to make logical sense. If you don't remember your dreams, that's okay! Building this relationship doesn't always happen overnight (pun intended). Keep practicing, and soon it'll become second nature.

DREAM JOURNALING QUESTIONS

What did you feel immediately upon waking? Take note of any feelings, even something subtle like confusion or uncertainty. How do these feelings relate to your waking life?

Did you have any dreams? If so, record them with as much detail as possible, paying special attention to any colors, symbols, numbers, themes, or people that stuck out to you. If you do not remember your dream, that is okay. Know that your subconscious is working in the background, even if your conscious mind isn't aware, and look out for any signs or symbols during the day that pertain to your dream requests.

Incorporating rest as a part of your overall development is an integral part of staying Unruly. Rest asks you to slow down, be more present, and ultimately reminds you of your humanity, which can be easily forgotten in the fast-paced, results-driven world we live in. Rest is the final tool in your Unruly toolbox. As you move forward in redefining, recreating, and molding your life, demand space and time to rest. You will need this, as the path you've chosen requires a concerted amount of energy, focus, and courage to embrace your intricacies out loud in a world that often coerces you to assimilate.

Repeat after me: It's okay to rest when I need to.

12

Keep Your Seams Visible

The Beauty Is in the Stitching

One of my friends is a magician—not in the David Blaine sense, but she can sit down at a sewing machine and construct a garment that previously only existed in her mind. I've always been in awe of how she can transform scraps of fabric into something beautiful through her imagination, intention, and labor. Before you know it, pieces of fabric become a bomb-ass outfit.

In garment making, the seam is an integral part of the construction of a garment, but the stitching that holds the various pieces together is meant to be hidden. The idea is for the eye to view one seamless garment with little attention to where the individual pieces begin and end. Alternatively, a designer can make the stylistic choice to purposely sew pieces of fabric together to create a visible seam, calling specific attention to the point at which the two pieces come together. The visible seam as I am referencing it here is a concept that was laid out in Nicole R. Fleetwood's book *Troubling Vision: Performance, Visuality, and Blackness*. She challenges the seamless narrative in digital media that seeks to make different elements blend together seamlessly. In her chapter "Visible Seams: The Media Art of Fatimah Tuggar," she argues that "the visible seam . . . highlights the contradictions, unintended consequences, and erasures in dominant cultural narratives."[1]

Whether or not you have the particular creative prowess of a seamstress, you too are a seamstress of a sort. Through healing, self-development, and deconstructing your identity, you are always figuratively negotiating seams and boundaries. You are always, at all times, either altering your garment or constructing a new one altogether. You gather scraps and make them into something useful and beautiful.

Your life is a patchwork. Being Unruly means choosing *not* to hide your seams. Resisting the urge to camouflage the contrasts within you that make you who you are. Throughout this book, you have put specific labor into acknowledging and making peace with aspects of yourself and your experience that don't seemingly go together. But lasting and profound inner harmony is created by a whole acceptance of your opposites. There's power in not fighting to keep up the illusion of seamlessness.

A couple years ago, sex educator and social media personality Shan Boodram publicly apologized for posting something on social media that she later learned was offensive to members of her community. She named what she said, cited why it was offensive, and apologized for the misstep. Up until then, I had never seen an influencer do that. By watching that interaction between Boodram and her audience, I learned the value in the visible seam. Instead of pretending that the misstep didn't happen, she highlighted it and owned it. This stitch became part of her visible seam, making her overall image even more relatable. The same goes for you. You give away some of your power when you allow shame to convince you to hide a mistake, to act like a perceived failure didn't happen, or to pressure yourself into being perfect.

Along your journey, there will be pressure to hide your seams, and that might work for some people but not for you. You are Unruly.

OUR FINAL WORKSHOP

The last day of The Unruly Retreat is always bittersweet for me. On one hand, I am completely full of love, joy, gratitude, and appreciation for the women and the experience I had the pleasure of hosting. And on the other hand, I feel the nagging reality that we're about to return to a world that won't be as kind and accepting as the one we've created together during this time. Our little world is coming to an end, for now.

As we prepare to leave the world we created and return to the Crooked Room, I like to call back to the Crooked Room activity we did during the first session. I ask all the women to stand up and try to balance on one leg. As they do, I can hear the shuffling of chairs and bodies moving, the excited voices of the women.

"Close your eyes," I instruct them. "Take a moment to notice what your body is doing to support you being balanced. What do you notice?"

"Well, I know what to expect now, so it's not that hard," one woman said.

"This is easy depending on how many cocktails you have," another interjected.

Looking around the room, I saw them intently focused on balancing, some more solid than others. From far away, someone might look like they're balancing perfectly still, but up close, you realize that their body is trembling, making a series of micro-movements to maintain standing on one leg. Similarly, seeking balance while maintaining your Unruly-ness in your real, everyday life will also require a series of micro-movements. And keeping your seams visible is also a practice in mobility, flexibility, and courage. It's a practice of making micro-adjustments each and every day to become the best version of yourself, one decision at a time.

Unruly Inquiry

Think back to the aspirational, future version of yourself you described at the beginning of the book. With everything you've learned, how receptive are you now to this version of yourself? If you've become more receptive to her, which tools have resonated with you the most? If you're still feeling hesitant, what do you think is standing in the way?

BE TRUE

I invite you to resist the urge to make your seams perfect and invisible. Resist that urge to flatten yourself out, water down your humanity, and hide your inner diversity. Your goal is not to be accepted. Your goal is not to be understood. *Your goal is to live out your truest story.* In these moments of self-realization, I think about all the brilliant woman minds, like bell hooks, whose feminist texts are categorically misrepresented even though she went out of her way to painstakingly detail how much of her work advocated for men's humanity as well as women. I think about how much she fought for the greater good of the entire collective, only to be purposely misunderstood, even after her death. I think about Nina Simone, who ended up leaving the United States just to find safety and solace. I think of my mom, who never got the kindness that she needed. I think of my sister, who was never given the protection she deserved. I think of all the women I've worked with that share a similar experience. Desperately seeking to be seen, heard, and understood by the world. As hooks put it, "Before I could demand that others listen to me I had to listen to myself, to discover my identity."[2]

Their perseverance, dedication, and bravery paved the way for you and me to step into our greatness unapologetically. My hope is that my book has allowed you to give yourself everything this world hasn't (yet). Your goal—no, your *responsibility*—is to live your life in the most authentic, real, and honest way possible. I pray that you continue to speak to yourself, to hear yourself, and to allow yourself to be seen. You deserve to realize your deepest desires and become the woman of your dreams—in fact, you are already there. You are a part of this new Unruly world, and even though we might not be able to live in it all the time—for now—we are actively creating it so that generations to come can benefit from it. Shifts are happening, and you are a part of that.

I honor you for going on this journey with me. I wish you happiness, health, and liberation as you continue the process of unlearning, unfixing, and unbecoming. May you live life with you in mind first and foremost, may you go forth with a new perspective, and above all else, may you stay Unruly.

Repeat after me: I am unapologetically Unruly!

BONUS
Metta Meditation Exercise
(Based on a Teaching by Steven Smith[1])

I use this meditation as a closing activity for my retreat and I want to do the same for you. This section is modified slightly from Steven Smith's original teaching. Loving-kindness, or metta, as it is called in the Pali language, is unconditional, inclusive love, a love with wisdom. As Bart Mendel puts it, "Metta meditation was taught by the Buddha 2600 years ago and is still practiced in many traditional Buddhist communities to this day, just as he taught it."[2] It has no conditions; it does not depend on whether one "deserves" it or not; it is not restricted to friends and family; and it extends out from personal categories to include all living beings. There are no expectations of anything in return. This is the ideal, pure love that everyone has the potential to give and receive. To experience this level of metta, we must begin by loving ourselves, because if we do not have a measure of this unconditional love and acceptance for ourselves, it is difficult to extend it to others. Only then can we include others who are special to us—and ultimately, all living things.

To help us find our metta in this moment, let's do an exercise. Settle into a comfortable position. Breathe normally. Focus on the sensations of the breath coming in and out of your body, entering and exiting your heart's center. Repeat these phrases silently to yourself.

May I be happy.
May I be healthy.
May I be free from danger.
May I live life with ease.

Next, think of a person who you'd like to extend the feeling of pure unconditional loving-kindness to, the kind of love that does not require anything in return. This person may be someone you consider a mentor or elder. They might be a parent, grandparent, teacher—someone it takes little effort to respect and revere, or someone who immediately elicits the feeling of care. Imagine that person sitting calmly and quietly across from you, and know that they, just like you, just want to be happy.

Repeat the phrases for this person:

May you be happy.
May you be healthy.
May you be free from danger.
May you live life with ease.

After extending strong unconditional love to your person, allow them to leave, waving or hugging them goodbye if you wish. Now, move to a person you regard as a dear friend, someone whose company you really enjoy. Imagine them sitting calmly and quietly across from you, and know that they, just like you, just want to be happy.

Repeat these phrases for this person:

May you be happy.
May you be healthy.
May you be free from danger.
May you live life with ease.

Allow this person to slowly fade away, waving or hugging them goodbye. Now, move to a neutral person, a stranger, someone for whom you feel neither strong like nor dislike. Maybe it's someone you saw at the grocery store, in your apartment building, or during your daily commute. Imagine this person sitting calmly and quietly across from you, and know that they, just like you, just want to be happy. As you say the phrases, allow yourself to feel a deep sense of care for their welfare.

May you be happy.
May you be healthy.
May you be free from danger.
May you live life with ease.

Allow this person to slowly fade away, waving or hugging them goodbye. Now move to someone you have difficulty with, someone who you find it difficult to feel loving-kindness for. This person could be an enemy or any person you feel strong, difficult emotions toward. Imagine this person sitting quietly and calmly across from you and know that they, just like you, just want to be happy. Repeat the phrases for this person.

May you be happy.
May you be healthy.

May you be free from danger.
May you live life with ease.

If you have difficulty doing this, before the phrases, you can say, "To the best of my ability, I wish that you be happy/healthy/free from danger, etc." If you begin to feel ill will toward this person, visualize your benefactor and let the loving-kindness arise again. Then return to this person. Let the phrases spread through your whole body, mind, and heart.

May you be happy.
May you be healthy.
May you be free from danger.
May you live life with ease.

Return it back to yourself.

May I be happy.
May I be healthy.
May I be free from danger.
May I live life with ease.

Allow this loving-kindness feeling coming from your heart center to expand into your immediate surroundings. Send this love to everyone in your home, in your neighborhood, in your city, your state, throughout the United States, the entire continent and the world. Include every living being on this earth. If you'd like, continue to expand your loving-kindness, using it to fill the endless emptiness of the universe. Repeat these phrases for all beings.

May all beings in the air, on land, and in the water be safe, happy, healthy, and free from suffering.
May all living beings everywhere, on all planes of existence, known and unknown, be happy, be peaceful, be free from suffering.
All awakened ones.
All seekers.
All humans.
All those who feel the weight of oppression.
All forms of government and judicial systems.
All those who are no longer on this earthly plane with us as we know it.

We send unconditional loving-kindness.
And to you I say:
May you be happy.
May you be healthy.
May you be free from danger.
May you live life with ease.

Notes

CHAPTER 1: THE WORLD IS YOUR STAGE

1. Carl Jung, *Psychology and Alchemy* (Princeton, NJ: Princeton University Press, 1968), 20.

CHAPTER 2: SETTING THE SCENE FOR SAFETY

1. Resmaa Menakem, *My Grandmother's Hands: Racialized Trauma and the Pathway to Mending Our Hearts and Bodies* (Las Vegas, NV: Central Recovery Press, 2017), 62.

2. Melissa V. Harris-Perry, *Sister Citizen: Shame, Stereotypes, and Black Women in America* (New Haven, CT: Yale University Press, 2011), 28.

3. Justin Michael Williams and Shelly Tygielski, *How We Ended Racism: Realizing a New Possibility in One Generation* (Boulder, CO: Sounds True, 2023), 115.

4. Menakem, *My Grandmother's Hands.*

5. Henry Louis Gates, Jr., "How Many Slaves Landed in the U.S.?" PBS, accessed February 26, 2024, pbs.org/wnet/african-americans-many-rivers-to-cross/history/how-many-slaves-landed-in-the-us/.

CHAPTER 4: MAIN CHARACTER ENERGY

1. Kendra Cherry, "The 6 Types of Basic Emotions and Their Effect on Human Behavior," VeryWell Mind, December 1, 2022, verywellmind.com/an-overview-of-the-types-of-emotions-4163976.

CHAPTER 6: SELF-LOVE IN ACTION

1. Nathaniel Branden, *The Six Pillars of Self-Esteem* (New York: Bantam, 1994), 92.

CHAPTER 7: PASSED-DOWN PERFORMANCES

1. Andrew Samuels, Bani Shorter, and Fred Plaut, *A Critical Dictionary of Jungian Analysis* (New York: Routledge, 1986).

2. Jainish Patel and Prittesh Patel, "Consequences of Repression of Emotion: Physical Health, Mental Health and General Well Being," *International Journal of Psychotherapy Practice and Research* 1 (2019): 16–21, doi.org/ 10.14302/issn.2574-612X.ijpr-18-2564.

3. Bruce D. Perry and Oprah Winfrey, "Connecting the Dots," in *What Happened to You? Conversations on Trauma, Resilience, and Healing* (London: Bluebird, 2022).

4. Meeri Kim, "Study Finds That Fear Can Travel Quickly through Generations of Mice DNA," *Washington Post*, December 7, 2013, washingtonpost.com/national/health-science

/study-finds-that-fear-can-travel-quickly-through-generations-of-mice-dna/2013/12/07/94dc97f2-5e8e-11e3-bc56-c6ca94801fac_story.html.

CHAPTER 8: PRESENCE OVER PRESENTING

1. Sanford Meisner and Dennis Longwell, *Sanford Meisner on Acting* (New York: Vintage Books, 1987).

2. Christy Gibson (@tiktoktraumadoc), "Using #iffirmations Instead of #Affirmations Can Be Easier If You've Been through #trauma #PTSD #cPTSD," TikTok, June 18, 2021, tiktok.com/@tiktoktraumadoc/video/6975242371155954949?lang=en.

CHAPTER 9: WHAT'S YOUR NEXT SCENE?

1. "Goldilocks Zone," Exoplanet Exploration, NASA, accessed March 28, 2024, exoplanets.nasa.gov/resources/323/goldilocks-zone/.

2. "Video: Breathing Exercises: 4-7-8 Breath," drweil.com, accessed March 25, 2024, drweil.com/videos-features/videos/breathing-exercises-4-7-8-breath/.

CHAPTER 10: CASTING FOR COMPANIONSHIP

1. Laurie Santos, "Why Americans Are Lonelier and Its Effects on Our Health," interview by John Yang, *PBS NewsHour*, January 8, 2023, pbs.org/newshour/show/why-americans-are-lonelier-and-its-effects-on-our-health.

2. Amy Novotney, "The Risks of Social Isolation," *Monitor on Psychology* 50, no. 5 (May 2019): 32, apa.org/monitor/2019/05/ce-corner-isolation.

3. Joy Harden Bradford, *Sisterhood Heals: The Transformative Power of Healing in Community* (New York: Ballantine Books, 2023), 145.

CHAPTER 11: A DRAMATIC PAUSE

1. Carolyn J. Rosenthal, "Kinkeeping in the Familial Division of Labor," *Journal of Marriage and Family* 47, no. 4 (November 1985): 965–74, doi.org/10.2307/352340.

2. molly_west (@molly_west), "My mom's life changed when I taught her about this. #feminist #feminism #mentalhealth #mentalhealthawareness #genderrole #genderexpression #education #kinkeeping," TikTok, December 30, 2022, tiktok.com/@molly_west/video/7183168131706178858.

3. Christopher Chabris and Daniel Simons, "The Invisible Gorilla Experiment by Harvard University," theinvisiblegorilla.com, Accessed 18 Apr. 2023, theinvisiblegorilla.com/gorilla_experiment.html.

CHAPTER 12: KEEP YOUR SEAMS VISIBLE

1. Nicole R. Fleetwood, "Visible Seams: Gender, Race, Technology, and the Media Art of Fatimah Tuggar," *Signs: Journal of Women in Culture and Society* 30, no. 1 (2004): 1429–52, doi.org/10.1086/421888.

2. bell hooks, *Ain't I a Woman: Black Women and Feminism* (New York: Routledge, 2014).

BONUS

1. "Loving Kindness Meditation," Mysticism and Spirituality Circle, April 15, 2021, mysticism-spirituality-circle.com/loving-kindness-meditation/.

2. Bart Mendel, "Getting Started with Metta Meditation," Mindworks, accessed October 25, 2023, mindworks.org/blog/getting-started-metta-meditation/.

About the Author

Shelah Marie is an author, storyteller, and CEO of Curvy, Curly, Conscious. An advocate for unruly women everywhere, Shelah empowers and educates her attendees, audience, and readers to challenge their beliefs about themselves, embrace their full expression, and make choices from a place of aligned authenticity. Please visit shelahmarie.com for more information.

About Sounds True

Sounds True was founded in 1985 by Tami Simon with a clear mission: to disseminate spiritual wisdom. Since starting out as a project with one woman and her tape recorder, we have grown into a multimedia publishing company with a catalog of more than 3,000 titles by some of the leading teachers and visionaries of our time, and an ever-expanding family of beloved customers from across the world.

In more than three decades of evolution, Sounds True has maintained our focus on our overriding purpose and mission: to wake up the world. We offer books, audio programs, online learning experiences, and in-person events to support your personal growth and awakening, and to unlock our greatest human capacities to love and serve.

At SoundsTrue.com you'll find a wealth of resources to enrich your journey, including our weekly *Insights at the Edge* podcast, free downloads, and information about our nonprofit Sounds True Foundation, where we strive to remove financial barriers to the materials we publish through scholarships and donations worldwide.

To learn more, please visit SoundsTrue.com/freegifts or call us toll-free at 800.333.9185.

Together, we can wake up the world.